Here's what others say about
SMART VIDEOCONFERENCING

"This book provides unique and pragmatic insight into communication using videoconferencing. In today's world where many are trying to define new strategies to deal with geographic separation and time sensitive issues, *Smart Videoconferencing* is essential reading."
—CRAIG DINSELL, EXECUTIVE VICE PRESIDENT, OPPENHEIMER FUNDS

"*Smart Videoconferencing* is so full of wit and wisdom, it should be read by every executive whether or not they ever use videoconferencing. Janelle Barlow, Peta Peter, and Lewis Barlow have compiled not only the most intelligent and most readable book on this subject, they've also brought together the most extraordinarily useful set of tips on public appearance etiquette I've ever read. This book may also be one of the funniest business books in recent memory. Many of the stories that accompany each of the authors' dozens of tips are so hilarious they'll make you laugh out loud. And the pronunciation guide at the end of the book is alone worth the price of purchase. I know you'll love this book as much as I did!"
—JIM KOUZES, COAUTHOR, *THE LEADERSHIP CHALLENGE* AND *ENCOURAGING THE HEART*, CHAIRMAN EMERITUS, TOMPETERS!COMPANY

"With this book the authors have been able to create the perfect guide on how, when, and for what to use videoconferencing. *Smart Videoconferencing* clearly states all shortcomings people have encountered using any method of conferencing. If I had had this book five years ago, I might have had a positive attitude toward videoconferencing."
—PAUL SPIERINGS, TECHNICAL SERVICES MANAGER, BRITISH TELECOM IGNITE SOLUTIONS, AMSTERDAM

"Unless you've read *Smart Videoconferencing*, the results of your next videoconference will either be (1) memorable, (2) without impact, or (3) so bad it is now a part of your legacy. This handbook guarantees your results. A 'must' read for every executive."
—THOMAS GRISSEN, COO, MAXIMUS

"A significant contribution to the world of communication. The book is cogent, informed, and very readable. A must for all businesspeople."
—GRANT D. MELDRUM, SENIOR VICE PRESIDENT, THE ZIMMERMAN AGENCY

"This book is a must-read for anyone curious about videoconferencing or seriously planning to do more with it. Application of the concepts here can save you untold problems from mispronouncing words, goofs on screen, and more. It is filled with practical, real-world examples that can help you avoid problems that others, even celebrities, have encountered."
—TERRY L. BROCK, "TECHNOLOGY TOOLS" AND "CYBERSENSE" COLUMNIST

"*Smart Videoconferencing,* very enjoyable to read with its amusing anecdotes to illustrate its points, dispels the myths and technical complexity of VC in a user-friendly guide. This book will make a busy executive's life immensely easier and less stressful."
—NIGEL ROBERTS, GENERAL MANAGER, GREAT EAGLE HOTEL, HONG KONG

"If your company uses videoconferencing or is considering this technology, read this book! *Smart Videoconferencing* gives executives all the tools they need to look and sound their best in this new medium."
—KAREN LAM, PRESIDENT, COMPASS INTERNATIONAL

"*Smart Videoconferencing* takes you step by step through the do's and don'ts of this powerful media. If you want to master videoconferencing, you must read this book."
—NIALL MURRAY, DIRECTOR OF TRAINING AND DEVELOPMENT, THE VENETIAN RESORT, HOTEL, CASINO

"I didn't realize how much I didn't know about videoconferencing etiquette. I went from clueless to confident in one plane ride!"
—JENNIFER WIMMER, EVENTS COORDINATOR, PIONEER INVESTMENT MANAGEMENT, INC.

"In the light of how many corporations now want to use VC as a way to not travel and yet discuss business issues proactively, this book will make a significant impact on virtual meetings."
—Leon Enriquez, Editor, *I.T. Times*, Singapore

"As both a ready reference and a checklist, *Smart Videoconferencing* will help you gain 'that competitive edge' in videoconferencing. This book is one of those 'must-haves' in the executive library!"
—Imad Elias, Corporate Vice President, Rotana Hotels, Suites and Resorts, Dubai, UAE

"Through their helpful hints, the authors draw your attention to the many potential pitfalls of videoconferencing. Using this book as a guide, you can get the results you're looking for."
—Jane Devries, Human Resources Information Systems Administrator, John Deere Credit, Burlington, Ontario, Canada

"A highly practical manual for the 'hands on' type of manager. The clever reader can put their best foot forward and create *bella figure* the next time they hit the airwaves. Particularly useful for international readers is the glossary of commonly mispronounced words in English."
—Ruth Ann Lake, partner, Focus Consultants, Milan, Italy

"In the years ahead, we'll all spend more time communicating via video. *Smart Videoconferencing* is a perfect blend of practicality and entertaining stories that illuminate. It's the benchmark guide for this essential business tool of the future."
—Bob Treadway, Futurist

"One of the toughest challenges in business communication is to connect with people both emotionally and intellectually. When you can't look into a person's face directly, it is even more of a challenge. You need this extremely important book."
—Patricia Fripp, author and presentation coach to America's CEOs

"You simply cannot afford to look bad in your virtual meetings, and *Smart Videoconferencing* will give you all the tools you need to both look and communicate at your best."
—DANIEL BURRUS, TECHNOTRENDS

"*Smart Videoconferencing* is a must read for any organization currently using or contemplating using videoconferencing as a mode of communication."
—KELLY BLASHER, EPHIBIAN EVANGELIST

"Substantive and practical from beginning to end. This is the only book you need to read for all your on-camera videoconferencing needs."
—NIDO R. QUBEIN, CHAIRMAN, GREAT HARVEST BREAD COMPANY, FOUNDER, NATIONAL SPEAKERS ASSOCIATION FOUNDATION

"This is the only reference book leaders will need to make sound business decisions on how and when to use videoconferencing."
—PATRICIA ZAKIAN TITH, PRESIDENT, GLOBAL WORKPLACE

"This book does an exceptional job of highlighting common video conference disasters, and offers insightful, practical tips for avoiding them. Make this excellent resource your organization's standard."
—BRUCE SCHEER, PRINCIPAL, FUTURESIGHT CONSULTING, SEATTLE

"Emotional intelligence is the centrepiece of human communication and interpersonal relations, and this innovative book adds a new dimension to these very valuable skills. It is a must-read for those who want to more effectively and professionally get their message across to others."
—REUVEN BAR-ON, PH.D., MANAGING DIRECTOR, EMOTIONAL INTELLIGENCE RESEARCH LABORATORY, CO-EDITOR OF THE *HANDBOOK OF EMOTIONAL INTELLIGENCE*

"All work is theatre. Unfortunately, too many workers behave no differently on stage than in their private lives. *Smart Video-conferencing* literally puts a spotlight on such poor performances. We hope many executives and managers will read this book in an effort to strengthen their remote acts."
—B. JOSEPH PINE, II AND JAMES H. GILMORE, AUTHORS, *THE EXPERIENCE ECONOMY*

Smart
Videoconferencing

Smart
Videoconferencing

New Habits for Virtual Meetings

Janelle Barlow

Peta Peter

Lewis Barlow

BK

BERRETT-KOEHLER PUBLISHERS, INC.
San Francisco

Berrett-Koehler Publishers, Inc.
235 Montgomery Street, Suite 650
San Francisco, CA 94104-2916
Tel: (415) 288-0260   Fax: (415) 362-2512   www.bkconnection.com

ORDERING INFORMATION

Quantity sales. Special discounts are available on quantity purchases by corporations, associations, and others. For details, contact the "Special Sales Department" at the Berrett-Koehler address above.

Individual sales. Berrett-Koehler publications are available through most bookstores. They can also be ordered direct from Berrett-Koehler: Tel: (800) 929-2929; Fax: (802) 864-7626; www.bkconnection.com

Orders for college textbook/course adoption use. Please contact Berrett-Koehler: Tel: (800) 929-2929; Fax: (802) 864-7626.

Orders by U.S. trade bookstores and wholesalers. Please contact Publishers Group West, 1700 Fourth Street, Berkeley, CA 94710. Tel: (510) 528-1444; Fax: (510) 528-3444.

Berrett-Koehler and the BK logo are registered trademarks of Berrett-Koehler Publishers, Inc.

Printed in the United States of America

Berrett-Koehler books are printed on long-lasting acid-free paper. When it is available, we choose paper that has been manufactured by environmentally responsible processes. These may include using trees grown in sustainable forests, incorporating recycled paper, minimizing chlorine in bleaching, or recycling the energy produced at the paper mill.

Library of Congress Cataloging-in-Publication Data
Barlow, Janelle, 1943–
  Smart videoconferencing : new habits for virtual meetings : be
your best on camera, save time, save money, get better results /
by Janelle Barlow, Peta Peter, and Lewis Barlow.
    p. cm.
Includes bibliographical references and index.
ISBN 1-57675-192-9
1. Videoconferencing. 2. Business communication—Technological
innovations. 3. Business etiquette. I. Peter, Peta, 1948– II.
Barlow, Lewis, 1968– III. Title.
HF5734.7.B37 2002
658.4'56—dc21   2002021562

Copyediting and proofreading by PeopleSpeak.
Book design and composition by Beverly Butterfield, Girl of the West Productions.

FIRST EDITION
07 06 05 04 03 02   10 9 8 7 6 5 4 3 2 1

Contents

Preface   ix

Acknowledgments   xv

Introduction   1

PART ONE: WHAT'S IT ALL ABOUT?

1   Videoconferencing: A Twenty-First Century
Business Tool   9

2   Why New Habits Are Needed   17

3   Limitations of Videoconferences   25

PART TWO: HABIT 1—LEVERAGE YOUR CHOICES

4   Should Your Meeting Be a Videoconference?   36

5   The Demands of Videoconferences   38

6   Videoconference or Face-to-Face Meeting?   40

7   Videoconference or Teleconference?   42

PART THREE: HABIT 2—THINK PRIME TIME

8   Preparation   46

9   Interesting Agendas   48

10   Setting Personal Agendas   50

11   Getting a Great Start   52

12   Moderators   54

13   Question Handling   56

14 Importance of Participation 58

15 Watching Your Time 60

16 International Videoconferences 62

17 Strong Closings 64

18 Following Up 66

19 Lessons Learned 68

PART FOUR: HABIT 3—MAKE TECHNOLOGY YOUR FRIEND

20 Microphones 72

21 Cameras 74

22 TelePrompTers 76

23 Lighting 78

24 Taping 80

25 Documents 82

26 Murphy's Law 84

PART FIVE: HABIT 4—MAXIMIZE YOUR PRESENCE

27 No Food, No Gum 88

28 Distractions 90

29 Patterns and Colors in Your Clothing 92

30 Anger and Other Negative Emotions 94

31 Assume You're Live 96

32 The Importance of Being on Time 98

33 When You Are on a Panel or Part of a Group 100

34 Makeup 102

35 If You Are Sick 104

36 Jewelry 106

37 Your Voice 108

38 Controlling Your Nerves 110

39 Your Eyes   112

40 Your Hair   114

41 Your Clothing   116

42 Grooming   118

43 Your Gestures   120

PART SIX: FINAL CONSIDERATIONS

44 A Videoconference Checklist   125

45 A Legal Caveat   129

46 The Future of Videoconferencing   131

Appendix A Storyboarding   135

Appendix B 105 Commonly Mispronounced Words   137

Notes   149

Bibliography   151

Useful Terms to Know   153

Index   165

About the Authors   171

We dedicate this book to the people who had the vision
to persist beyond the earliest prototypes of
videoconferencing systems. We honor those lone individuals
who excitedly sat in darkened sound-proofed booths squinting
at blue light and photoelectric cells to claim success
when they could barely make out a dim and fuzzy image
of another human being they were talking to.
We also cheer those individuals who kept a clear vision
of what videoconferencing could be even while they laid
lines sometimes consisting of more than twenty linked
regular telephone lines to transmit almost stationary images.

They are the pioneers in the field and without their efforts
and vision, we would not enjoy the sharp, crisp, almost
natural images we can see today while videoconferencing.

Preface

We, the authors, have participated in excellent videoconferences that have left us breathless with the possibilities of this medium of communication. We have also participated in virtual meetings that made us shudder, cringe, and wonder if the world is ready to use this technology successfully.

We have written this book to share our more than forty years combined experience in training people how to run better meetings, make exciting presentations, and look good in front of cameras. Our goal is to help our readers avoid easy-to-make mistakes. These blunders not only detract from the effectiveness of videoconference meetings; mistakes also make people nervous about using videoconferencing (VC) and will therefore slow down the inevitable widespread use of videoconferencing in the business world.

Our lives have been spent in front of groups and in front of cameras; we have been interviewed hundreds of times on television. We have spent countless hours researching techniques that make people look effective. We know what works. And we also know what prevents people from leveraging this new medium of communication.

Once we understood the dynamics of the trends identified in chapter 1, we checked the literature to see what was available to help people create new habits that would take advantage of videoconferencing and appreciate the differences between in-person meetings and videoconferences.

We found precious little on the subject, and nothing that addresses the topics in-depth that are covered in this book. For example, a recent article by an interactive media consultant outlines seven steps for a "successful videoconference"—but never once mentions anything about presentation style. While we do not question the necessity of someone in the organization taking responsibility for technical aspects of setting up VC systems, these "steps for successful videoconferencing" have little to do with how individuals appear, perform, and leverage their time during the videoconference meeting itself. This particular list, and others like it, could apply equally well to successful implementation of Web browsers or e-mail systems.

When organizations experience failed videoconferences (or "video meetings" as they are sometimes called), even when the failure has nothing to do with the equipment, they tend to be gun-shy about approaching VC again. And they frequently do not like to admit it. Executives at a major retail company (who prefer to remain unidentified), for example, tell us they are unlikely to use their expensive VC equipment again because of poor experiences. We doubt their resolve will last. If nothing else, at some point their suppliers will force them into virtual meetings.

But these bashful retailers illustrate an important point. The technology has now reached the stage where picture and sound quality give VC many of the qualities of live, face-to-face meetings. In order for people to accept this newest communication device, however, they must look good and be positively rewarded for their participation. In order for this to happen, businesspeople must learn the skills necessary to perform well in front of a camera. Because of its current high quality and its obvious ability to save time and money, VC will become widely used if we can avoid presentation failures.

We do not recommend that people set standards that demand "perfect" videoconferences. After all, a meeting is a meeting, and if you are too concerned with looking good on camera, you may appear tense. However, because of the inherent power of being able to simultaneously transmit voice, visual images, and interactive data, avoiding failures is essential and demands that we acquire new habits for our videoconference meetings.

Videoconferencing is only one type of virtual meeting, a broad term that includes e-mail, data collaboration, Webcasting, Web conferencing, online chats, and white boarding. This book focuses solely on videoconferencing and the new habits that have to be learned in order to perform well when you can both see and verbally interact with others at another remote site in real time. Businesspeople today may videoconference right in the middle of another type of virtual meeting, such as when they are data collaborating. The skills available to readers of *Smart Videoconferencing* can definitely be applied to even the most minimal on-camera interaction.

New Habits for Virtual Meetings

Part of the challenge of VC is getting people to understand the unique aspects of videoconferencing technology. David Carlson, president of Affinity VideoNet in Essex, Massachusetts, puts it this way: "The hardest thing with videoconferencing is changing people's habits."[1] Many people believe that a videoconference is the same as an in-person meeting except that it is accomplished from distant locations, and that they, therefore, do not need to do anything different than they would at an in-person meeting.

Based on dozens of interviews with users of VC technology, we have observed that people regularly make assumptions about videoconferencing—assumptions that unfortunately result in less-than-effective videoconferences. Many assume

- That they should schedule a videoconference simply because they have the equipment.

- That they can "wing" their virtual meetings in the same way they frequently prepare for their in-person meetings.

- That all they have to do is show up for their meetings and they will be able to work effectively with VC equipment. This equipment can be your friend if you know a few things about it; it can also be your enemy if it is misused.

- That what they see and hear in person is what their remote sites are seeing on their monitors. In fact, the way we act in front of a camera is amplified to remote site attendees and may not look at all like what you experience in person.

This book will introduce you to four solid habits—Habit 1: Leverage your choices, Habit 2: Think prime time, Habit 3: Make technology your friend, Habit 4: Maximize your presence—that address these faulty assumptions. The habits, which follow the introduction and three background chapters on videoconferencing, are tested and easy to implement. They will help you look your best, avoid the above pitfalls, and ensure that permanent records kept of your meetings will make you look good for a long, long time.

Each of the habits begins with a "big premise" that conceptually organizes the content that follows. The first habit, on leveraging your choices, helps you think through your options about whether or not to hold a videoconference. Habits 2 through 4 offer dozens of tips and ideas, which are explained with real-life examples.

If you are tempted to read the introduction and then immediately skip to the four habits, we strongly encourage you to return to the first section of the book entitled "What's It All About?" The information there will add depth to your understanding of the role of VC in today's modern business society.

The Need for Face-to-Face Meetings

We believe, along with many experts in the industry, that videoconferencing will never eliminate the need for face-to-face business meetings, particularly meetings with customers. Negotiating contracts or competing for major sales requires us—in most cases—to show up in person. In-company meetings will undoubtedly be most impacted by this new world of VC. Even then, the most important in-company meetings and the ones that have team building as a main purpose will still need to be held in person. We predict that eventually videoconferencing will be seen as adding value to other communication media rather than simply taking the place of in-person meetings.

Achieving added value will require sophisticated staff who know how to present on camera. We listened to the marketing director of a high-tech company describe her first videoconference. The camera was already on as people entered the room for a project meeting to which the marketing director had been invited. She was confused about where to sit and what to do. She had not been given instructions on how to act or what to wear, and she felt very exposed. The room was harshly lit with overhead lights so that deep shadows appeared on her face. Sunlight flashed through scanty blinds, making halos of bright white light float around the room. When she later watched a tape of the meeting, she was horrified by her appearance on the monitor. As she said, "It ruined the experience."

She is not inclined to try again, and that is a shame. Not only will she miss out on all the benefits of videoconferencing, but it did not need to be that way.

Las Vegas   JANELLE BARLOW
June 2002   PETA PETER
                                                              LEWIS BARLOW

Acknowledgments

Upon beginning a project like *Smart Videoconferencing,* there are many anxious moments spent wondering if a germ of an idea can turn into a book. As the book continues through its many stages, it becomes a community affair. Finally, it becomes a finished project that represents untold numbers of hours offered by people who can never be sufficiently thanked.

We have made friends through this process. Our anxiety was relieved when we came to realize the material we wanted to share was already being asked for by businesspeople around the world. The process of discussing videoconferencing made us feel as if we were on a new frontier—which in fact all users undoubtedly are! Some video-conference users are old hands at virtual meetings, but most are just beginning to learn new videoconferencing language that makes for particularly far ranging and exciting conversations.

To all the people who read drafts of this book, answered our questions, gave us feedback, advised us on technical issues, tolerated our schedules, and even our moods—which would not always be appropriate to share in a videoconference—we are eternally grateful. Every comment was carefully considered, and if we have made any mistakes, the fault lies totally with us. It should be noted that not everyone we talked with agrees with each other!

Our gratitude goes to Pamela Fedderson whose insight made us rethink every sentence in this book; Jeffrey Mishlove who continues to support every book project conceived of by the TMI author team; Stuart Cohen who read through several drafts of the book with incisive comments on every read; Terry Brock and Vin D'Agostino who sparked our creativity; Julie Gouldin and Simon Moyer of Tandberg;

Jay Koenigsberg and Claire Millsap of Vexcorp (Jay is a shining star in this new world of videoconferencing); Brooke Ysteboe of InView and Carole Hodges of WorldCom (who lent their advice and help on numerous occasions in hopes that our book will promote the field of videoconferencing); Todd Cadley at Sterling Hager and Nicole Burdette at O'Keeffe & Company; Karen Pugsley at Newberg High School in Oregon; Clare Richardson-Barlow who gave us numerous examples of how Generation X is currently using virtual communication; Bernie DeKoven, for wonderful and long discussions on the challenges of meeting planning; Leigh Levy and Peter Skovrup at Compunetix; Bruce Eaton at Pacific University for stellar technical advice; David Gold of Acoustic Communications; Paige Salazar, training director at InView, who really understands the challenges of videoconference meetings; Andrew Davis and Andy Nilssen at Wainhouse Research for straight and to-the-point statistics; Roompam Jain at Frost and Sullivan, who wasn't bothered by our incessant e-mails; our Australian friends Scott Page with Ipex Information Technology Group, and Clive Allen and Kimberley Winters, both with Telstra ConferLink. We also thank our TMI colleagues Bill Oden, Elcee Villa, Jennifer Schmicher, and Ralph Simpfendorfer. Our reviewers were mercifully kind in their comments and gave us tremendous feedback on our early drafts: Karen Lam, Bob Schiffman, Terry Linda, and Michael P. Scott. To the many people who wrote testimonials for us— thank you! Their comments are reprinted at the front of this book. Rita Rosenkranz, our agent, has once more guided us through the book publishing world. Our final thanks go to the incredible team at Berrett-Koehler. Steven Piersanti, publisher, immediately understood the significance of this work, and everyone on his team has been generous, supportive, and filled with ideas that have inspired us in our thinking about the virtual and the real world. We look forward to videoconferencing with them.

Special thanks to the Las Vegas Athletic Club for being open twenty-four hours so we could find a healthy way of relieving our stress after those late nights at the office and to the Red Rock Country Club swimming staff. They have kept that pool clean for us!

Introduction

In its simplest terms, videoconferencing involves individuals sitting in front of video cameras, talking with and viewing each other on monitors, much as they might if they were in the same room together. They may also look at or work on electronic documents during their videoconference. The medium is real-time interactive, and far-end participants can both hear and see each other. The compelling reason for holding a videoconference is to intensify human interaction without having to travel.

We recently met the marketing director of a major manufacturer of videoconferencing systems. We shared personal stories, got to know each other as much as is possible in an initial meeting, covered our agenda, set tasks for both sides to complete, and established a time for our next meeting. We laughed, enjoyed ourselves, and commented on how good we all looked. The only unusual feature of the meeting was that the authors were in Las Vegas, Nevada, while the marketing director was in Reston, Virginia.

However, if you talk with seasoned business professionals about videoconferencing, you will not always hear of such successful virtual meetings. Jill Addams, an executive coach, is frequently asked to help clients who have paid a price for assuming their current in-person meeting habits will work with videoconferences. Jill describes a top-level manager with years of business experience who lost a significant job opportunity because he thought that his in-person meeting skills would be adequate to showcase his talents in a videoconference.

This highly skilled businessman interviewed with a company that uses videoconferencing extensively with international virtual teams. He was told that VC skills would be a critical part of his job description. He was also told that he would be asked to participate in an actual videoconference as a part of his job interview process. "How different can VC be from a regular meeting?" he told Jill. He did not prepare for the unique challenges of VC, violated most of the principles of effective on-camera work, and failed the interview miserably.

A few years ago, the type of situation described by Jill would not have occurred. But now we are in a new world where videoconferencing is becoming a communication device commonly used by organizations—large and small. Managers working with virtual teams are *expected* to know how to effectively use the medium.

Consider concierge Anna Morris of the Westin Hotel in Santa Clara, California. Most would think that a concierge would have to conduct work in person, but Anna works via videoconference from her home, saving her a lengthy daily commute. A large monitor is set up in the lobby of the Westin, where Anna "virtually" assists hotel guests. In her home, Anna sits in front of parallel videoconferencing equipment and a backdrop resembling the Westin lobby. She does everything a regular concierge does—answering questions, calling for restaurant reservations, and faxing driving directions. Anna insists the guests pay closer attention to her on video than they ever did when she worked on-site.[2]

Businesspeople today use videoconferences for a multitude of purposes, including

- Holding monthly marketing meetings in companies with multiple locations

- Holding regular meetings for virtual teams, especially international teams

- Narrowing down a field of candidates for a position

- Holding annual board meetings required by law

- Showing product samples sourced in distant locations to local offices

- Introducing new employees to field offices

- Training staff and customers interactively

- Holding shareholder meetings (in those states where this is legal)

- Conducting regular discussions of monthly financial figures at multiple sites

- Demonstrating products to customers

- Staging multisite conferences so attendees in different parts of the world can simultaneously see and interact with the speakers

In the future, VC will use miniature cameras mounted on a variety of products, including mobile telephones, automobiles, PDAs (personal data assistants), and even watches.

Data Collaboration and Web Conferencing

A lot of people today use interactive technology to collaborate on data. Data collaboration allows people in remote locations (or even down the hall from each other) to electronically share documents on a computer monitor—even making changes or notations to the document at the same time. Data collaboration can be a part of a videoconference meeting. However, most people who use data collaboration never use cameras. Obviously, this type of virtual meeting is less expensive. It is appropriate to think of data collaboration as a distinct application of videoconferencing that does not require the use of a camera.

Web conferencing refers to a set of software applications (e.g., WebEx, PlaceWare, and Paltalk) that use Web technology to host meetings or presentations. With such Web conferences, the camera feed is only unidirectional, though voice and written communication can go in both directions.

For example, one stock market expert simultaneously watches a live real-time Webcast of the Nasdaq Stock Exchange with day traders around the United States who use his software. On another monitor, the expert makes verbal and written comments about what is happening in the market in order to educate his users. Participants in the session ask questions and comment—into microphones attached to their computers—so everyone hears everyone else. These particular

Web conference sessions do not use cameras to transmit human images.

Data collaboration can be much more elaborate than the above example, and VC can play a role. Consider a group of consultants, well equipped with video cameras, who are working on a proposal that requires immediate feedback and input from colleagues located in a different city. Because both groups need to see the document simultaneously, a telephone call or e-mail would be less effective. The lead consultant checks to see who is available and pushes a button to connect to the sister office. Once connected, both groups can see each other while they are focused on their electronic proposal. The image will be small, however, because their monitors will primarily be occupied with data.

When the two groups want to brainstorm ideas or draw diagrams, they use a white board visible to both parties. If they need input in the middle of their session from another colleague, who lives in Japan, they can connect to his cellular telephone through their computer and bring him into the meeting via voice. Toward the end of their meeting, the consultants may want to update a senior exective about their project's progress and "see" her reaction. The executive happens to be traveling. They contact her; she sets up her laptop computer, plugs a small inexpensive camera into her computer's USB (universal serial bus) port, and joins the virtual meeting for ten minutes. While the primary purpose of the meeting was data collaboration, videoconferencing made nonverbal information available and also added the dimension of human connectivity to the meeting.

Data collaboration and Web conferencing demands are entirely different from those of videoconference meetings where people primarily want to see each other while talking with each other. When people use data in videoconferences, they use PowerPoint, Excel, or Web demonstrations primarily to illustrate points they are making. Incidentally, Webcasting is different from data collaboration and Web conferencing in that there is usually no communication exchange at all—people watch a video presentation that is streamed over the Internet.

Data collaboration is document focused and tends to be more casual. People generally do it at their desks from their computer monitors; they typically do not use a meeting room. While dual-monitor systems make it possible to keep visual contact with a remote site on one monitor (using the second monitor for document viewing), it is much more common in data collaboration to use a single computer monitor. In such cases, people who share data see each other only at the start of their meetings—if at all—since the documents they share will occupy most or all of the space on their monitors.

Even the brief viewing that may occur in a data conference, however, could very well have two lasting effects on the whole field of videoconferencing. First, people will become increasingly comfortable with the "looking at each other" aspects of virtual communication. This will, in turn, make data conferences feel incomplete unless people have a live, albeit brief, opportunity to see each other as part of the communication exchange. In the future, people will likely complain about telephone calls or data conferences that involve data transmission only, saying, "You know, we should have videoconferenced so we could see each other."

Videoconferencing Technology

Because videoconferencing means different things to different people, a book on the subject potentially has a lot of ground to cover—which in part helps to explain why many videoconferencing books are very thick. *Smart Videoconferencing* definitely does not cover every aspect of the topic. We include a VC glossary to cover basic technology terms, but we do not cover technical aspects of VC in detail. We also do not cover how to data collaborate. Our focus is on *how to present yourself.*

Many excellent books, articles, and white papers (a bibliography is attached) cover everything you will ever want to know about VC technology. It is our belief, however, that, beyond acquiring a working vocabulary, most users of VC, like most users of the telephone, are not that interested in how it works—but in whether it works. What you need is a grounding in the "how to use it" aspects of the technology. For example, you need to know how to turn your equipment on, how to fix basic problems, including how to reboot or restart, and how the whole system works together.

Most manufacturers of videoconferencing equipment provide excellent technical training. Usually you can ask the manufacturer's technicians to conduct a practice virtual meeting with you. The company's goal is for you to feel comfortable with its equipment and experience first hand what the equipment can do. We definitely recommend using services like this. This type of practice session allows you to learn the fundamentals of your system so you can concentrate on your presentation when you get ready to hold your first virtual meeting.

Finally, from a technical point of view, you also need to understand that in order to have a good videoconference exchange, you need (1) top-notch equipment, (2) adequate bandwidth to transmit video, data, and audio information, and (3) equivalent equipment and bandwidth at the receiving end.

Break any one of these links, and, from a technical point of view, you will have a less than optimal videoconference experience. If you have sophisticated equipment but your remote site does not, do not count on a great virtual meeting. In the same way, if you have invested heavily in elaborate equipment but have inadequate bandwidth to transmit data, you will not have the stellar results that are possible.

Looking good on camera and participating effectively in virtual meetings is imperative in today's world for whatever reason you hold your virtual meeting or how extensive your equipment is. Our tips and strategies will help you develop good habits for looking your best at the most demanding levels of videoconferencing. Nonetheless, even if you only send your image to one other remote site so you and a colleague can "glance at" each other before you begin to collaborate on an electronic document, the practices in this book will help you look good on camera and provide you with ideas to improve your day-to-day virtual meetings.

PART 1

What's It All About?

Videoconferencing: A Twenty-First Century Business Tool

For many, it was the highlight of the 1964 World's Fair in New York City. People waited in the heat in long lines at the AT&T Pavilion to talk with—and see at the same time—a stranger from another fair location. The Bell Labs' Picturephone was, more or less, successfully demonstrated to the public. People were excited. Many were convinced—or told—the future had arrived.

Videoconferencing had actually been around for decades. It was first demonstrated by Bell Labs technicians who displayed a crude link between Washington, D.C. and New York City in the 1920s. Those in the know hoped this visionary medium would soon realize its potential. It did not. Even after the 1964 World's Fair excitement, videoconferencing failed to have broad usage for another thirty years.

Now at the beginning of the twenty-first century, VC technology has dramatically improved, and bandwidth continues to be more affordable. Futurist and columnist for BizJournals.com, Terry Brock, sees even bigger changes on the horizon: "Telephone lines will go the way of the dinosaur. All communication will eventually go over the Internet, and we will definitely see videoconferencing ease-of-use that equals personal computing today."[3]

Affordable bandwidth is fueling the demand to be able to see people while talking with them over long distances. Forecasts from the two leading research firms in this field suggest that the worldwide market for virtual services and videoconferencing systems is growing dramatically. Wainhouse Research predicts that worldwide tele-, video-, and Webconferencing *services* will grow from $2.8 billion in 2000 to $9.8 billion by 2006.[4] Researcher Roopam Jain at Frost and Sullivan projects that worldwide revenues from the sales of group and desktop systems for videoconferencing will grow from $574.3 million to $1.54 billion by 2006.[5]

The demand for VC services is being felt around the world. Videoconferencing systems were first offered in Japan in 1984. Demand for them has grown rapidly ever since, even in a country where time spent together in person is considered essential. In 1988, 250 systems were installed; in 1993, 3000; in 1995, 8800; in 1998, 80,000; and in 2000, 320,000.[6] When charted, the impressive growth curve looks like this:

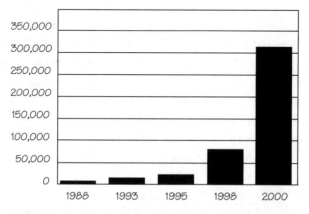

If these figures hold true, they imply that videoconference equipment and systems will become as common as fax machines. Businesses will be forced to use the technology or look as outdated as companies without fax machines did in the late 1980s.

We attribute this heightened need and interest in videoconferencing to four trends that are turning videoconferencing into a necessary communication tool for business instead of merely a clever way to meet someone virtually. Furthermore, the convergence of these four trends is spurring predictions that upwards of 50 percent of meetings in the next decade will involve some type of video transmission.[7]

Trend 1: Videoconferencing Technology and Quality Will Continue to Improve While Costs Drop

From its first—and failed—commercial application by Bell Labs in 1964, videoconferencing technology has come a long way. Bob

Schiffman, of Kelley Communications in Las Vegas, proudly demonstrates the latest equipment available from Tandberg, considered to be the Rolls Royce of the industry. It is very high quality, and Bob will tell you it is reasonably priced. Tandberg produces a dual-monitor system that can connect to as many as ten remote sites, affording simultaneous video and data presentations. Bob says that software upgrades have significantly enhanced both the speed and quality of Tandberg's product line. In fact, all VC equipment is getting better, and prices have dramatically fallen.

Consider what has happened in VC technology in just the last few years. The majority of VC systems now have "touch-button" capability so they immediately connect to other systems. Prior to this capacity, people had to take several steps in order to connect. Users can now spontaneously add someone to their virtual meetings; they can surf the Web in the middle of their interactions; and they can stream video for all participants to view.

Desktop systems are available that can connect through USB ports, with "plug and play" capacity; that is, the computer will not have to be restarted after connecting. Prior to this development, connecting through one's desktop involved considerable technical expertise and time. As a result of the convenience of plug and play, the phenomenon of personal videoconferencing has dramatically increased.

Recent technology has also significantly increased the quality and "realness" of video images. For example, "3-D" videoconferencing, offered by Dallas-based Teleportec, now takes "virtual reality" to a new level. Teleportec has a product that projects images onto a thick sheet of glass embedded with light-reflecting particles. Users report that the images have a three-dimensional, or holographic, quality that make them more lifelike than a television screen, creating the sense that viewers are in the presence of a live human.

As higher quality videoconferencing equipment is achieved, along with lower prices, the number of users will increase and VC will continue to be easily and unremarkably integrated into the communication devices that managers, supervisors, and frontline workers use daily to conduct business. Videoconferencing is no longer just a means for senior executives to show off their latest electronic tools—

as it has been for some companies. For example, Polycom, the largest manufacturer of videoconferencing equipment, sells powerful and affordable equipment with as close to television quality that can be installed in four offices for less than $25,000.

Videoconferencing technology, using a wireless approach (which is currently available and growing in use), will allow users to view and participate inexpensively in conferences, meetings, and press conferences via the Internet from—a remote office, a car, while on a business trip to Shanghai or a vacation, or from a home office— almost anywhere. That is the vision. Furthermore, videoconferencing over the Internet will significantly leverage the investments companies have already made in their information technology (IT) infrastructures.

Trend 2: Controlling Costs and Saving Time Will Become More Critical in the Competitive Global Economy

Compared to the cost of sending a team any distance at all, the price of high-quality videoconferences has become very attractive. In fact, some companies are requiring their staff to explain—before scheduling a trip—why a videoconference would not work as well as an in-person meeting. Eighty-eight percent of a group of travel managers surveyed by the National Business Travel Association in late 2001 reported they will increase their use of VC to control travel costs. Compare that percentage to the one in a similar survey by the same association made six months earlier, when just 33 percent said they would use more VC to reduce their travel budgets.[8]

To companies that schedule several meetings each year and whose operations are in multiple locations, vendors of VC systems argue that the cost of the highest-end VC equipment can be earned back in a matter of two years or less. Admittedly, the manufacturers and distributors of VC equipment make a lot of strong statements so it is difficult to determine just how accurate such claims might be. For example, one industry spokesperson stated that just one use of a videoconferencing system could equal the cost of bringing people together!

Live video events, linked by satellite, that match television broadcast standards are expensive—but they are able to reach thousands of people. Prices for satellite conferences range from $5,000 to more than $175,000 per setup. Even prices at this level, however, represent substantial savings when compared to travel and housing costs for thousands of people. These video events can also reach huge audiences in multiple cities who otherwise would not attend. Major conferences of this type can now also be conducted over ISDN (integrated services digital network) lines with substantially lower costs. Janelle recently spoke to an audience in Ljubljana, Slovenia, while four ISDN lines beautifully carried her entire six-hour workshop to another group assembled in Skopia, Macedonia, who watched her on a gigantic screen. During that entire period, connection to the remote site was lost only once and was quickly reestablished.

A major selling point of VC technology for many companies is not so much cost savings as time savings. Because videoconferences tend to be more structured, meeting time may be more efficiently spent compared to meeting in person. When a product helps organizations complete work significantly faster than before, cost is automatically less important and the product is almost guaranteed to become widely used.

The authors, all frequent flyers, regularly overhear businesspeople moan about productive time and family time lost to travel. For example, on a flight from Los Angeles to Seattle, Lewis Barlow heard a salesman from Rhinotek Computer Products calculating that with flying time, check-in, security, and travel to and from the airport, the trip ate up a full eight hours—all for a half-hour meeting.

And every "road warrior" has his or her own disaster stories of wasted time. Darr Fedderson, a well-respected business executive, laments, "When I worked as the national accounts manager for Rustoleum Paint, a colleague and I flew from Portland to Texas, with a plane change in Denver. When we arrived at Garden Ridge's office, the key decision maker was absent because of a family emergency that took place while we were traveling." Fedderson and his colleague had to make the same trip the following week. If a videoconference had been scheduled and canceled, the time wasted would have been minimal.

We have flown across the United States (losing a day in the process) and stayed overnight to participate in an hour-long sales meeting the following morning—in a jet-lagged state of mind. We then spent an equal amount of time returning home. Granted, these can be necessary and very lucrative meetings, but that is a heavy investment of time in order to participate in a one-hour meeting, and not all of these meetings need to be conducted in person.

Time and costs can be saved in other ways—only limited by one's imagination. People who locate products for distributors around the world can connect with customers via VC and show their products immediately instead of shipping samples. Individuals can show, buy, and sell used automobiles to distant buyers via videoconferences. Decisions can be made more quickly, and products get to stores and customers faster. This means time can be saved and productivity is increased.

Trend 3: Businesspeople Will Develop More Flexibility in Their Use of Communication Technologies

Long-distance communication has expanded dramatically since smoke signals and carrier pigeons. Now most competent businesspeople know how and when to use e-mail, faxes, PDF (portable document format) and graphic files, hard-copy letters, mass mailings, voice mail, cellular telephones, and person-to-person meetings. Most salespeople, for example, know when to pick up the telephone and talk with a customer, when to send an e-mail, and when a personal visit is necessary.

Videoconferencing enables businesspeople to contact more clients and colleagues in a shorter period of time. For example, a manager might be aware of two or three important meetings in locations across a wide geographical area that the manager could add value to by attending. Videoconferencing would make these multiple meetings in multiple locations possible in one day.

Videoconferencing also allows people to communicate with each other in a way that is perceived to be more connected than a simple telephone call. For example, the authors attempted to sell our consulting services to a software company. We knew that just talking over the telephone would not lead to the kind of business relationship we wanted. At the same time, we knew we did not have a good enough relationship with the company to request an in-person meeting. We proposed a meeting using VC. The human resources (HR) director agreed. Being able to see each other on-screen allows people to become more familiar and comfortable with each other, leading to business that would probably never happen without the use of VC as one of the tools in the communication arsenal.

As more people become comfortable with videoconferencing and know how to maximize their time in virtual environments, requests for videoconferences instead of in-person meetings will become commonplace. Salespeople will not *automatically* be expected to travel thousands of miles in order to have a chance at getting an order. In our own training and consulting business, we now hear with increasing frequency from our large corporate clients, "Shall we videoconference about that?"

Business customers are becoming more guarded with their time as their workloads increase. Various studies already show that many customers prefer immediate access to their vendors over in-person contact. In other words, they will accept a videoconference in place of an in-person meeting—if they can schedule it right away.

Research conducted by a major consulting firm shows that, since 1970, business customers have shifted dramatically in what they say is necessary to complete a deal. Being able to have face-to-face contact with a company representative was the number one factor that companies specified in 1970. By 1990, however, this factor dropped dramatically—to eighth place![9]

Companies need to evaluate the impact of videoconferencing on their customer relationships. Videoconferencing may give organizations, even small ones, a new and less time-consuming more reasonably priced way of reaching out to memorably touch their customers. Any kind of meeting that allows people to see each other, even if it is not in person, can be a strong pull for repeat business.

Trend 4: Protecting the Environment and Conserving Resources Will Become Even More Important Considerations

Although environmentalism is now a minor factor pushing the demand for VC, it appears to be a growing one and is already important for environmentally conscious organizations. A majority of the population now believes that global warming is more than speculation and is concerned about it. In addition, an increasing percentage of people have a heightened sensitivity to their own impact on the environment. They will choose alternatives in order to avoid adding more pollutants to the environment.

Even if they are not avid conservationists, many organizations try not to waste precious fuel sources and pollute the atmosphere. Companies today recycle paper, aluminum cans, and bottles. They have accepted the ban on smoking indoors. And they often reason that a videoconference is less damaging to the environment than moving dozens of people around in airplanes and cars.

When socially conscious individuals see the strong links between saving time and costs and helping to protect the environment, this trend will be one more consideration that is factored into the decision whether to hold a person-to-person meeting or to schedule a videoconference.

Videoconferencing at the Tipping Point

These four trends are creating a "tipping point," to use the term popularized in the book by the same name.[10] A tipping point, as described by author Malcolm Gladwell, is a phenomenon that occurs when a critical mass is achieved. When a social practice has "tipped," it actually drives its own expansion. Because videoconferencing is on the brink of this critical mass point, businesspeople, need to be ready for a complete integration of VC into their lives.

While it is tempting to focus on the technology of videoconferencing, we will better leverage our time spent in virtual meetings if we take a people-centered approach to this newest communication equipment and focus on the new habits needed to take advantage of it.

Why New Habits Are Needed

We have come a long way from simply being excited about seeing people who are far away while talking with them to turning the technology into a necessary business communication tool.

Without developing the best habits, however, it is possible—even likely—we will completely misuse this visual medium, look awful, and be perceived in a negative way. And because videoconferences are easily recorded, any mishaps can be watched hundreds of times.

Jay Koenigsberg, founder and CEO of Vexcorp, Inc., a private IP (Internet protocol) network of videoconference services, has set up a network of branch locations across the United States. Jay points out, "The videoconferencing experience is either good or bad. There are no in-betweens."[11] In addition to providing centralized scheduling, and top-notch easy-to-use VC equipment, Vexcorp adds value by paying attention to what Koenigsberg calls the "total videoconference experience." Vexcorp has experimented with paint colors on his studio walls and settled on a deep blue that is best projected across the public Internet. Chairs do not rock or swivel. Lighting is soft. All of the locations have their city site listed with the Vexcorp logo. This enables participants to easily identify the location of each speaker. These are small details, but they matter. Koenigsberg describes one of his competitors who set up a VC studio in a strip mall next to a Virginia beach. Everyone could see people walking by in bathing suits through the glass window positioned directly in the camera's view.

Unique Aspects of Videoconferencing

Videoconferencing shares one salient characteristic with public relations, television broadcasting, and public speaking: good habits increase a person's effectiveness in front of an audience. And developing these habits to a point where you do not have to think about them can make the difference between success or failure.

Historians have noted that military officers tend to fight current wars as if they were still engaged in their previous battles. Likewise, most of us use the latest technology as if it were a mere extension of a previous medium. If we assume that videoconferences are merely regular meetings transmitted by video, we will be like those military generals who failed to appreciate the full applications of tanks and airplanes in warfare. We will underutilize VC and fail to appreciate the damage a poorly run video meeting can do to individuals and teams.

We all know that people have many bad face-to-face meeting habits. They waste time. They do not take advantage of the opportunities that a group of people can create in real space together. In face-to-face meetings, people interrupt each other; that can create chaos in a videoconference. People display negative body language—body language that will be amplified in a videoconference and recorded on tape for repeated viewing. People come unprepared to regular meetings, a practice that is more visible during a videoconference. The mere introduction of a camera makes any videoconference meeting more formal than an in-person meeting. Any problems that exist with regular meetings will be highlighted with VC. In addition, an entirely new set of problems will occur. As a result, more discipline is required to make virtual meetings effective.

Videoconferences also require structure especially when multiple sites are involved. If decision making in your organization primarily occurs during side conversations or in the hallways at meeting breaks, do not expect that to happen in videoconferences. Videoconferences may speed up decision making, but this can work against you because speed can result in the failure of all parties to accept the decision and therefore actually slow down implementation.

While several people can see each other during a videoconference, only one person at a time can hold forth or people will end up electronically talking over each other. In addition, if the system has a voice-activated camera that focuses on the speaker, interruptions can create chaotic movement as the camera jumps from one person to the next. When someone stops talking, a three-second delay may occur before the next person's remarks are activated. This slows the broadcast down. As a result, people need to follow a fairly orderly process or visual and auditory elements can be disruptive. To minimize the interruption problem, some videoconferences assign a person to control the switcher (an electronic device that allows only one person to be broadcast at a time).

People talking over each other commonly happens during any type of meeting. We are able to mentally sort out this very human style of communication when we are all in the same room together. The challenge is to manage this style virtually across multiple and distant sites.

Most in-person meetings also do not get recorded; a videoconference is easily captured. When together, people can readily see who else is in a room; one cannot assume that everyone in the room is visible on camera during a videoconference.

People and their organizations need to view videoconferences as a unique form of communication. Aspects of VC need to be determined by the culture of the organization, the sophistication of the equipment available, and the reasons why the virtual meeting has been scheduled in place of an in-person meeting.

Videoconferencing is not as reliable a form of communication as the telephone, at least at the beginning of the twenty-first century. The telephone nearly always works—even for teleconferences set up at multiple sites. However, it is not uncommon for VC sessions to be disconnected or run into other technical problems. Fortunately, once a conference is disconnected, it is fairly easy to start it up again. Virtual meetings require patience, which most of us do not possess, accustomed as we are to the stability of wired telephone connections.

Demonstrations of desktop VC equipment at videoconferencing shows almost always look better than real usage. We have heard the complaint, "Try connecting it to a *real* network," from everyone except people who sell the technology. VC experts also emphasize that low-end (in other words, more affordable) technology simply does not match the consumer's expectations of VC's capacity.

While we cannot specifically predict how VC will eventually develop, we will point you in the right direction as you use the medium. We will help you think about and begin to develop habits that may make the difference between advancing your career and putting the brakes on it. It is probably a good idea to get off on the right foot with new habits—when you are on camera!

You're on Television—Act Like It

In many ways, videoconferencing is similar to much of today's broadcast journalism. CNBC financial shows, with their informality, resemble what an in-house conference might look like. And CNN's *Town Meeting* show, complete with e-mails sent in for a moderator to respond to, are close to what we can expect many in-house videoconference events to be like in the future.

While we may excuse business virtual meetings that are not quite up to CNN standards, we still have high expectations for anything that is on video. Virtual meetings that look as if someone put a stationary video camera in front of a group of people and set the lens at wide angle will be unacceptable. People who could not attend the meeting and are expected to watch such a video record will be very unhappy—and very bored.

This resemblance to television scares many people about VC. They feel exposed and they do not know how to match television standards. After all, others—who are not in the room with them—are watching them and possibly making negative side comments! By comparison, people on television business channels have had years of experience in developing habits to look professional. Television broadcasters know how to keep the viewers' interest; they shift frames, run multiple pictures simultaneously, and talk in sound bites. Videoconferences are interactive—unlike television programs. They use conversation to work ideas, consider pros and cons, and gain support. They do not engage in these activities to entertain or attract a larger audience. While content is extremely critical in a business virtual meeting, it is easy to overlook the fact that the way the content "looks" can be equally important.

In one sense, being on television is easier than participating in a videoconference. Because broadcast cameras keep shifting frames and focus, no one is on camera all the time. However, in a videoconference when the camera lens is set at wide angle to include a group of people seated around the table, no one is ever off camera. In face-to-face meetings, we have the opportunity to scratch our heads, yawn, or stretch while colleagues focus on the person who is speaking. In a television studio interview, you are also blessed with commercial breaks. Videoconferencing, when you are *never* out of view, can be exhausting.

When tape recorders were introduced to the public, people squealed, "I don't sound like that!" when they first heard their voices played back to them. Today most of us are quite used to the sound of our voices on tape. Now you can hear people say the same thing, in effect, when they watch themselves on video: "I don't look like that" or "I hate my hair" or "That shirt looks horrible" or "Do I really look like that?" It's going to take us a while to become comfortable with seeing our images regularly projected back to us. And some of us may never like it!

Eventually, businesspeople have more or less learned how to adjust to all types of electronic communication gadgetry even though they certainly do not use all the tools to their maximum. Each type of new communication medium both generates and requires different habits. Voice mail, for example, required new habits—and some people still resist it and leave low-quality or unusable messages. Some of us excel at one medium over another, but we are all expected to have a minimal level of expertise with all means of communication and not to squeal like a teenager as we resist the medium.

Consider what would happen if you refused to use e-mail because you have difficulty writing your thoughts coherently in a rapid-message format. Although some senior-level executives get away with this because they have staff support, if they were just beginning their careers today they would never make it to the executive suite without using e-mail.

Some people do not like communicating by telephone, but in business you have no choice but to learn good telephone skills. Likewise, it does little good to complain about voice mail. You are going to run into it, so you need to know how to leave a succinct, appropriate message. Disliking cellular telephones is no excuse not to use them today. And if you refuse to deal with telephone "menus," you will never be able to get through to most organizations.

You had better have some degree of computer literacy in today's world as well. A decade ago some people would proudly raise their hands when asked who did not use a computer. Today, almost everyone (except for the very elderly) is too embarrassed to acknowledge an inability to use computer technology. You are expected to know how to download or upload documents, send graphic images, work a spreadsheet, and understand hundreds of acronyms.

VC is placing the same demands on businesspeople. A few years ago, few people would raise their hands in assent when asked whether they had ever participated in a videoconference. Now almost everyone indicates they have participated in a videoconference of some sort—or at least they are too embarrassed to acknowledge they have not.

FIGURE 2.1 VIDEOCONFERENCES COMPARED TO IN-PERSON MEETINGS

Videoconferences	In-Person Meetings
They are considered special events with a high level of excitement.	They are commonplace and frequently have a bad reputation.
Businesspeople need new habits.	Businesspeople can use old habits.
They are made possible by equipment.	Occur when people show up.
Tardiness and late starts are more noticeable.	People coming and going is usual.
You are always on camera unless your system switches the camera to different sites or people.	You face less personal scrutiny.
The benchmark is television.	No real benchmark exists except your organization's current meetings.
Tighter control of time because other people may be scheduled to use the equipment.	Tight control of ending times is not required.
Interruptions across sites create confusion.	Participants can easily interrupt each other.
They are easily recorded.	Recording requires effort and is noticeable.
They can be abruptly disconnected.	Human bandwidth does not normally disconnect!
Eating looks bad.	Eating is commonplace.
Managing the technology is critical.	The technology that must be managed is limited.
It is more difficult for everyone to speak.	It is easier for everyone to comment.
Negative facial expressions and body language are amplified.	Body language is part of total body communication.
Participants cannot necessarily see everyone.	Participants can easily see everyone in the room.
Side or hallway conversations are not easily conducted.	Side and hallway conversations are part of the total communication package.
You do not know what the other person is seeing.	You know what each other sees.

continued on next page

FIGURE 2.1 VIDEOCONFERENCES COMPARED TO IN-PERSON MEETINGS, *continued*

Videoconferences	In-Person Meetings
You only see what the camera focuses on.	You see the whole space in the meeting room.
Clothing patterns and colors make a difference.	The human eye can handle any color and pattern.
Sounds are amplified.	Many sounds get lost.
More people at multiple sites can be accommodated.	Meeting rooms have space limitations.
People can disappear from a meeting if they never talk and the camera is voice activated.	Everyone in a meeting can be seen, whether talking or not.
You need to learn to use some equipment.	You do not need to learn to use any equipment.
Side conversations will cause chaos if you do not have mute buttons and use them.	A softly spoken side conversation will not be disruptive.
Lots of bandwidth is needed to use video displays.	A VCR can easily be used.
More electronic applications are possible.	Fewer electronic applications are possible.
You can easily bring people from a great distance.	Bringing people is costly and time-consuming.
They require greater discipline and structure.	They require less discipline and structure.

Limitations of Videoconferences

No one believes or even suggests that videoconferences will replace face-to-face meetings. In fact, some people even doubt that this medium will be as widely accepted as we may first think. Their voices need to be heard in order for us to understand exactly how videoconferencing can add value to the mix of communication tools we currently use. The negative viewpoints will help us to think more clearly about maximizing the effective use of videoconferencing.

A common point of view is that videoconferencing will add value by supplementing telephone and written communication when more human connectivity is desired or required and in-person meetings are not possible or are too time consuming or expensive. Videoconferencing will sit between telephone and in-person meetings as another communication tool available to businesspeople.

Chuck House with Intel, for example, suggests that substituting a videoconference for an in-person meeting might be worse than skipping some meetings altogether. "Consistent remote attendance heightens frustration, builds alienation, and serves to segregate more often than integrate the remote attendee."[12] House's point is worth considering.

Several VC commentators agree with House's sentiment. They say it is difficult enough to know what is going on inside the heads of other people when you are with them. When you are watching a small, flat small image of someone, it is even more challenging. While videoconferencing attempts to create the impression that you are in the same room meeting face-to-face, you definitely are not. You cannot really look people in the eye. This is particularly true when dealing with a twenty-inch monitor with a screen split to view three or four locations. Details of faces are very difficult to see under these circumstances. As a result, we have to use the medium carefully instead of pretending it is something that it is not.

Electronic communication will always be different from person-to-person meetings. You cannot electronically transmit a handshake. Neither can you physically pat someone's back in a videoconference. You cannot transmit video images of everything that is happening in a group of people. You only see what the camera wants you to see.

Human communication is highly complex. And the transmission of images, whether across ISDN, DSL (digital subscriber line), or T-lines (high bandwidth lines used for videoconferencing), does not equal the real thing. Smells, the feel of another person's handshake, the opportunity to see the entire person with one glance, the ability to see the texture of the clothing the other person is wearing, body movements—all these contribute to our understanding of another human being.

This is why people frequently say that television never conveys the entire picture. The public heard that very phrase repeatedly after September 11, 2001, from visitors to Ground Zero, site of the World Trade Center twin towers. Apparently no television image (with the highest quality transmission links and the best cameras) came close to duplicating the experience of standing on the spot and viewing the extent of the destruction. Only by walking the entire perimeter of Ground Zero was one fully able to grasp the scale of destruction.

If you encounter someone in real life who is familiar from television, it sometimes takes a moment to be sure that the television image and the live human being are the same person. One of the authors recalls seeing former senator Bob Dole at a Washington, D.C., airport shortly after his defeat by Bill Clinton in the 1996 U.S. presidential election. Clearly, it was Bob Dole. But seeing him in person after viewing him for hours on national television was in no way the same experience.

In the same way, we have participated in videoconferences with individuals we had not yet met in person. In every case, we all agreed that we would probably not recognize these people if we saw them on the street amidst a crowd—especially if any time had passed.

This is because television is not three-dimensional. It distorts images. It provides incomplete visual fields. The colors are slightly off. Sometimes we only see head shots. Hand gestures may be unviewable. A video image is a pretty good facsimile, but it is not the real thing.

And make no mistake about it, videoconferences transmitted through ISDN or IP (Internet Protocol) lines, for example, while getting better all the time, do not provide the same crisp images afforded by a satellite link that beams regular television programming into our homes. And those images are where our expectations have been benchmarked. You can easily compare regular television cameras and Web cameras by watching CNN where, in a pinch, broadcasters will use a Web camera. The Web camera image is jerky, the voice and picture are frequently out of synch, and a noticeable time delay occurs between the anchor's question and the answer. The person on Web camera is waiting to hear what was said, and that delay lets us know this is not a normal television satellite link.

Communication Subtleties

Humans need the whole picture to assess reality. With a television image, we always wonder what is happening behind the camera. That is where we believe the real action takes places. We know that the picture transmitted on a screen does not show us everything. We only see television anchors dressed professionally—from the waist up. The anchor could be sitting with bare feet immersed in a pail of cold water to counteract the heat from the camera lights. (While Peta was anchor of an Australian television show, she witnessed this many times.) If we could see those feet in a bucket of water, we would have a very different impression of the television host.

It can be difficult to make important decisions without that up-close view. Business decisions are frequently made based on subtle gestures, a nod, or a grimace. When several people are in a room together, the interactions they have with each other all help the participants make up their minds about how to proceed. Two people glancing at each other at a pivotal point in a meeting can result in a decision to continue the discussion, a suggestion to pursue a particular point, or a contract—or not. These sorts of subtleties can be difficult to capture electronically in a virtual meeting.

Yet when you read current magazine and newspaper articles reviewing videoconference meetings, you are left with the impression that most people like them. Actually, liking it is never discussed. The assumption in these articles is that a meeting held in cyberspace was a success simply because it took place.

We question this. Janelle had an opportunity to participate in a client meeting that had live links to field offices in Latin America and other parts of the United States. A newspaper review of the event might have reported that a successful videoconference was held. We read about these "successful" videoconferences all the time.

From Janelle's perspective, the meeting, while technologically excellent, was a waste of time and money. No one felt engaged with the distant groups. The home office felt compelled to invite the people from the field offices to make comments so the group could feel as if everyone was participating. All the participation from remote sites did was slow down the entire flow and structure of the meeting. The first few connections to remote sites were interesting, but people in the local audience rapidly grew tired of them. Boredom settled over the group. Regrettably, we have heard this tale of boredom with VC repeated dozens of time.

Janelle participates in annual two-day planning retreats for the board of the National Speakers Association. These meetings could never achieve the same results they do using VC. Too much interactive communication is required to discuss the issues the board needs to address. Would VC be less expensive? Yes. Would it be as effective? It is extremely doubtful. Would it be the same as an in-person meeting? Definitely not.

In certain ways, telephone conversations and e-mail can be more intimate than a videoconference ever will be. The more information we have, the less the imagination is engaged. Think about the sound of someone's voice right in your ear. It is an intimate connection. You can hear the person's intonation and breathing across the telephone lines—even on wireless connections. It can be thrilling, even arousing. A teleconference enables an entire group to precisely hear each other's intensity, moods, and even health. That does not happen during a videoconference, in part because VC sound systems are normally not placed against the ear.

Even e-mail can be more intimate than videoconferencing. Two people sending instant messages back and forth or writing to each other in a chat room can create a sense of intimacy with words that the flat image of video misses.

If you want to watch up-close action at a football game, avoid sitting outdoors in the cold, and save a lot of money, then watching the game on television is a good choice. But to have an experience of the crowd, the excitement, the smell and taste of stadium hot dogs, you have to be in the stadium—even if you are sitting in the very top section of the stadium. In the same way, try celebrating Thanksgiving dinner with a videoconference. Or attempt to get a child to bond with you over video.

The news media used to comment on the "virtual dates" Bill Gates (before he married Melinda French) had with Ann Winblad, Silicon Valley's leading venture capitalist. Gates and Winblad would go to the same movie in different cities and then talk about the experience on their cellular telephones as they were driving home. Media commentators never knew quite what to say about these dates, as most people want a bit more contact than this on their dates. The media used the story to suggest that the very notion of "virtual" has changed us in subtle ways.

Human Bandwidth

John Perry Barlow, digital expert and cofounder of the Electronic Frontier Foundation, believes that the more interaction people have with virtual technologies, the more they will seek real interactions. Barlow says, "We know that there is no human condition with fatter bandwidth than face to face. We know that the more interaction people have virtually, the more inclined they are to seek face-to-face contact. It's a natural human instinct, to climb the spectrum of bandwidth."[13] In short, videoconferencing could do for face-to-face meetings what computers did for paper.

The promised paperless office never happened. All the computer did, with the help of prolific Hewlett-Packard (HP) printers, was to create more opportunities for people to quickly print out reams of material. In its own research, HP found that people do not feel they "own" a document on their computer screens until they hold a hard copy of it in their hands. Similarly, reading virtual books has nowhere near the appeal of reading a "real" book. It is hard to curl up with a PDA.

The frustration of the desire for in-person contact, erupting from what looks to be a guaranteed increase in videoconference meetings, may ultimately cause an increase in our desire to connect with each other in person. In short, limited communication breeds the desire for more complete communication. Virtual meetings may replace specific in-person meetings, but perhaps as some meetings are videoconferenced, even more face-to-face meetings will be scheduled.

Consider global teams. David Lewin, professor of management at the University of California, Los Angeles, suggests that up to 50 percent of global teams fail primarily because they do not have the opportunity to be with each other in person, where they can establish trust and learn each other's working styles.[14]

One of our Italian colleagues tells us about a very upset local client with whom she works. The American part of the team, located in California, calls the Italians when it is 8 P.M.—or later—Italian time. The Americans, who have not met the Italians in person, do not understand why their counterparts are not more enthusiastic during the videoconferences. Also, the meetings are held in English, which is normally difficult for the Italians, and speaking in a foreign language at 8 P.M. is even more challenging.

The Americans refer to the colors on the charts they are transmitting, even though they shaved the Italian budgets so the Italian team does not have the necessary electronic equipment to see the same colors. If the team had been established in person and these people knew each other personally before they began videoconferencing, more of the added value of VC might be easier to realize.

Senior-level businesspeople understand the need to have in-person time with people to find out who they are. They play golf with peers, spending hours with each other on the links, during which time many business deals are concluded. If this type of interaction is necessary for senior-level people to make good decisions, why should not the same thing be true for a junior-level person who works on an international product development team?

Putting people within video viewing range of each other spans distance. It does not tell people how much they can trust each other. Nor does a videoconference tell people much about their working styles. To realize the added value that VC can surely create, organizations must learn for what purposes they can most appropriately use VC. They also must know when they need to schedule face-to-face meetings.

Videoconferencing As a Complementary Service

Understanding the limitations of videoconferences enables us to now look at the value they can add. At times the nature of a discussion demands more human connection than a telephone call affords, but no opportunity exists to travel and meet in person. For example, in the authors' business we frequently like to converse with our trainers after they have completed a training program. We cannot meet in person, and the telephone is too remote. We would like that trainer out in a distant location, sitting in a hotel room, to feel connected to us and our home office. While not perfect, a videoconference call would be better than the alternatives. Ann Godi, president of Benchmarc Meetings and Incentives, argues that videoconferences will *supplement* telephone calls and teleconferences, while not eliminating face-to-face meetings. "I don't think face-to-face meetings are going anywhere. The more technology driven our industry is, the stronger the human need for meeting face to face," she says. At the same time, when used strategically, VC technology—because of the way it engages our vision—can take us closer to human connectivity than anything else.[15]

By understanding how to work with the limitations of videoconferences (a limited format when compared to one person meeting another person, face to face, handshake to handshake, in real space), you will be able to more appropriately and effectively use VC. The tragedy will be if we expect videoconferencing to accomplish the same tasks as in-person meetings. If so, we may dismiss this incredible medium by making demands of it that were never possible, and at the same time ignore some of the grand possibilities that are inherent in being able to push a button and see, in shared visual space, someone we are talking with who is hundreds or even thousands of miles away.

The three authors met with one of the companies that has a network of videoconferencing studios across the United States. We first met by telephone, and then by videoconference. This CEO—with a nearly infinite ability to videoconference—then suggested we meet in person!

The progression of communication was natural. The initial telephone conversation provided both parties with sufficient information about each other to know that we wanted more communication than a telephone call. Meeting in person would have been too precipitous. Videoconferencing became the next logical step. Both groups "passed the VC test," which made us suggest a face-to-face meeting. At the in-person meeting the dialogue was sufficiently in-depth so that we could clearly see where our relationship was headed.

We like a statement by Hugh Scrimgour, chief operating officer of Expocentric.com: "By no means do our services claim to be a substitute for the real thing. They are aimed at being a complementary service. But . . . they can be highly supportive as a way of keeping business communities together."[16]

PART 2

HABIT 1
Leverage
Your Choices

THE BIG PREMISE: VIDEOCONFERENCES
ARE NOT YOUR ONLY TOOL

As an old expression goes, if your only tool is a hammer, pretty soon the world begins to look like a nail. Once an organization has invested a couple of million dollars into state-of-the-art video-conferencing equipment, its leaders will feel a strong temptation to use it for everything.

But to reiterate the point made by Chuck House (societal impact and science policy director for Intel), holding a videoconference is not necessarily better than not meeting at all. House points out that the medium of videoconferencing itself will shape what happens in virtual meetings. For example, meeting in a videoconference could be viewed negatively if the participants believe a teleconference or a face-to-face meeting would have been more appropriate.

Perhaps a teleconference is the best tool for you to use. Interestingly, people pay closer attention in a teleconference than they do in a videoconference. The brain has to work harder in some ways to create images to go along with the spoken word. Video enables the brain to relax about the need to fill in gaps. This simple difference may lead participants (1) to assume they have heard things accurately in a videoconference when they have not and (2) to get bored more easily.

Habit 1 offers you a variety of ways to compare videoconferencing and alternatives so you can best leverage your choices. Our concepts are applicable in most cases. Yet for every principle we establish, we know there will be exceptions to our position. We encourage you to use this information to deepen your understanding of videoconferences, so when you do schedule one you will have made the best and most appropriate choice for you.

Should Your Meeting Be a Videoconference?

Meetings can be called for different purposes: brainstorming, listening to a speech, covering an agenda step by step, meeting the legal requirements of an annual board meeting, training, problem solving, collaborating on a medical decision, strategic planning, team building, introducing new people, reporting and updating, or selling.

Of course, not all meetings work well as videoconferences. For example, technical training seems to work very well in many virtual meetings, whereas staff motivation does not work nearly so well in a virtual meeting. Shared brainstorming among five different people across a huge geographical area is a clumsy use of VC, unless they go off-line to brainstorm and then come back to share ideas.

If this is your first foray into VC, give yourself time to learn from your own experiences. As you become more acquainted with video-conferencing, you can adjust and fine-tune your use of the medium. You will definitely go through a learning curve. Let every videoconference in which you participate be your teacher.

For example, one of our top-level clients in the hospitality industry recently installed video studios at most of the company's property sites. The clients initially thought they could use their new system for multisite meetings. Given their distinct rapid-fire style of communicating, however, they could not adapt to the time that was required to shift from site to site.

So, they have adjusted. Now they primarily use their VC system for conferences between two sites. That works for them. "It's practically as good as a regular meeting," they report, for planning budgets and sharing information on a monthly basis. Videoconferencing has dramatically reduced the amount of time the corporate executives have to spend on airplanes. And it saves them money.

Where they really deserve applause, however, is the way they have used the introduction of their VC system to think through how the medium influences all their meetings. They no longer automatically invite people to their annual or quarterly meetings, instead handling certain issues in virtual space. They have decided that just because someone holds a specific managerial position does not mean he or she needs to be at a meeting in person. This frees up budget resources to invite less-senior staff who normally would not get to attend these meetings, with the side benefit of creating status and learning experiences for the company's future leaders. Budget savings have also meant that the company can now schedule valuable in-person, team-building meetings for its cross-property teams.

5

The Demands of Videoconferences

One can definitely hold both informal and formal VC meetings. But generally speaking, VC meetings have a sense of formality attached to them as compared to a telephone call and even some face-to-face meetings. For this reason, videoconferences are great for formal speech and media presentation events, especially when involving multiple sites. These types of formal presentations require a great deal of preparation to be impactful.

Videoconferences between customers and suppliers require planning. Whenever you virtually meet customers, make sure your VC style matches your brand image. If you are at your desk computer, make sure that the video broadcast area is neat. Imagine the customers coming right into your office. What would they be able to see? What would you want them to see?

Multisite meetings that replace in-person working meetings also require a great deal of planning if they are to be an effective use of everyone's time. When you start to hold multisite meetings, get into the good habit of structuring them, especially when you know other participants have never taken part in a videoconference. One bad videoconference experience will create a negative impression that is difficult to shake.

One issue for leaders to consider is that VC can be so overused that its impact is blunted. The head of government, for example, must find the proper balance between keeping the public informed in times of crisis and being on television so frequently that the public fails to tune in to a special address to the nation. In the same way, heads of organizations who use multisite VC to set direction and motivate change across large organizations would be wise to space their videoconferences carefully so that when they occur, staff members know they are important. Save the splash of a multisite videoconference event for those occasions when you want impact.

WHAT DO YOU WANT TO ACCOMPLISH?

Answering the questions below can help managers and leaders make more effective decisions about scheduling virtual meetings or in-person meetings. "Yes" answers to the following questions suggest that a videoconference—with the appropriate level of technology—could help achieve and even enhance your objectives.

At times, controlling the results of the presentation may be critical. If so, ask yourself these questions:

- Do you want to highlight information? (For now, any announcement by videoconference is going to appear more significant than an announcement by almost any other means.)
- Do you want everyone informed at once?
- Is speed of the essence—particularly across a worldwide organization?

Perhaps you want to stress important concepts or pay tribute to special people. If so, these questions are relevant:

- Is it important to publicly acknowledge people and their achievements and have a permanent record of that?
- Do you need to reemphasize an idea, a target, a concept? (You have many options for emphasis in a video world: graphics, streaming video, music, size of screen.)
- Do you want to enhance the prominence of certain individuals? (Anyone given a presentation position will gain stature.)

Perhaps you need to reinforce your organization's culture. If so, ask yourself these questions:

- Do you want to inspire staff through regular weekly or monthly messages to adopt organizational culture change?
- Do you need your staff to be informed about decisions or changes going on in the organization?

6

Videoconference or Face-to-Face Meeting?

Sometimes you may have to choose between scheduling a videoconference or meeting in person. How do you make your choice?

Videoconferences

Videoconferences are more appropriate

- When executives already are popular and have high status. They do not need to shake everyone's hand to assert their position power.

- When you want groups of people at different locations to hear the same information simultaneously.

- When you want or need to save time and travel costs.

- When you want to involve people who might find it difficult to travel, perhaps because they are limited by weather, physical capability, or heavy schedules. For example, it is frequently easier to get an in-demand person to speak at a video event if he or she does not have to travel.

- When your far-flung staff has already worked together and can implement decisions as a team from distant locations.

- When you want the publicity that may be generated when the press learns you have held a major VC meeting. For example, Steve Jobs's videoconferences to Apple staff generate media attention.

- When you have time to adequately prepare for an elaborately produced virtual meeting so that your permanent record of it is something of which you are proud.

- When the content of your meeting does not demand that people have informal time with each other.

- When you want to introduce an important member of your team to your organization spread across the world.

- When you want a record of a virtual meeting for someone else to view, a history of your marketing and public relations efforts, or an uploaded link on your Web site for shareholders to view.

Face-to-Face Meetings

Face-to-face meetings are more appropriate

- When you have high needs for security and privacy. Some government agencies have the capacity to hold highly secure videoconferences, but most businesses run the risk of uninvited eavesdroppers.

- When participants may potentially hijack your videoconference by airing the organization's dirty laundry or creating factions.

- When you want to strengthen personal relationships.

- When a critical deal is being negotiated or closed.

- When you anticipate cross-talk and a lively, fast-paced exchange.

- When an important part of your meeting is the dialogue and interaction that goes on during or in between meeting sessions.

- When relationships are sensitive or unstable; for example, if you have a business customer or staff member who threatens to leave.

- When you absolutely do not want your meeting recorded.

- When you are making an announcement about a sensitive issue, such as downsizing, a merger, an acquisition, or a hostile takeover.

- When you doubt that an important member of your team will project well in a videoconference.

- When you want to make an event out of signing a contract.

- When your client says, "I'd prefer to see you in person."

7

Videoconference
or Teleconference?

Sometimes you have the choice of scheduling a videoconference or a teleconference. The following points will help you choose the best alternative.

Videoconferences

Videoconferences are more appropriate

- When you want or need a visual impact.

- When you want a conference that is more formal.

- When you need to work on electronic documents that everyone can see simultaneously and modify together.

- When you are making a statement about your organization with the medium of communication you have chosen—namely, that you are a big enough company to have in-house videoconferencing equipment; you have moved beyond teleconferencing; you are on the leading edge of technology.

- When participants need to connect names to faces.

- When participants want more visual cues.

- When participants have not seen each other in a while.

- When you want to shake up the routine from your normal teleconference.

Teleconferences

Teleconferences are more appropriate

- When you need to organize a meeting hastily. (Teleconferences, in many cases, are easier to arrange than videoconferences.)

- When greater flexibility is required in terms of when people enter and leave the meeting.

- When your meeting is less formal.

- When cost is an issue. (Teleconferences are less expensive today than videoconferences unless you are running your videoconference on the Web.)

- When you want everyone to pay closer attention. It is easier for participants to lose interest in a videoconference than a teleconference, particularly if participants participate minimally.

- When you only have access to one-way videoconferencing and you need to hear people's reactions.

- When you require a faster discussion exchange with quicker responses and the ability to interrupt.

- When people simply will not be available to meet by video.

- When you want an exchange that will less likely be recorded— the law requires that you get everyone's permission to tape-record a telephone conversation.

- When you have an identified moderator who can keep the discussion on track.

- When you need to set up an interactive meeting for people at a large number of sites. (You can easily arrange high-quality teleconference connections among people who are in fifteen different locations. That is more difficult with videoconferencing—at this point.)

PART 3

HABIT 2
Think
Prime Time

THE BIG PREMISE: DON'T WING IT

A lot of people think of the medium of television as shallow. As a result, many senior-level businesspeople have a fear of dealing with the news media. They know that many of their messages are simply too complex to explain effectively in ten-second sound bites. They correctly believe that their remarks can be easily distorted. They do not know how to be authentic while on camera. They suspect they do not have good on-camera habits.

While no one easy solution to these legitimate concerns exists, we need to accept the fact that we live in a media culture and understand that one effective way to meet the demands of that culture is to be well prepared. "Winging it" or improvising is simply not the way to approach a medium that has the potential to be broadcast to thousands of people, of which permanent visual records can easily be made, and which carries with it the prestige of and automatic comparison to network television. We must think prime time!

Preparation also requires respecting the limits of human communication. Vin D'Agostino, president of BNS Solutions, a consulting group in Walpole, Massachusetts, points out that when we have all our senses available to us (sight, smell, hearing, touch, and taste) we tend to get sloppy in our communication patterns precisely because we have so much information available to us.[17] Since videoconferencing comes closest to duplicating the senses we normally experience with in-person communication, D'Agostino notes that when videoconferencing, people tend to assume the same sensory conditions exist as in person. Obviously they do not, and as a result messages frequently do not come across in a videoconference. Avoiding the potential missteps of this assumption requires thinking your communication requirements through before beginning your videoconference.

8

Preparation

In order to hold a successful videoconference, you need to know the answers to a set of preparatory questions. Get into the habit of asking these questions before every videoconference except the most casual or informal.

- What is the purpose or objective of my virtual meeting? Is it a formal or informal conference? (Answers to these questions will determine the type of equipment you need and the amount of time you need to schedule. Informal conferences may be likened to two people running into each other in the hallway and having a conversation about work. Informal virtual meetings, generally conducted from personal computers, do not require the same attention as formal videoconferences.)

- What type of VC equipment do I have available to me? What do I need in order to achieve the objectives of my conference?

- Will the necessary VC equipment be available when I need it?

- What connections are possible on the other end of my conference? (You may have very sophisticated equipment while the other site has limited equipment.)

- How much time do I have for setup? (Some organizations schedule usage of their equipment so tightly that if a virtual meeting runs long, the entire schedule is compromised.)

- Will I have technical support available if I run into problems?

- What is the optimal number of participants? How many will be active participants and how many will be observers? (Obviously, you can have thousands of passive participants without a problem. Active participants—unless their only role is to transmit e-mail questions and comments—should probably be limited to the number you would invite for an effective in-person meeting.)

- How much experience do my conferees have with videoconferencing?

- Are there any special people I should invite to sit in: stakeholders, subject matter experts, senior executives, customers, suppliers?

SET REASONABLE EXPECTATIONS

Whenever a new technology is introduced, it is easy to oversell it. This is especially true of videoconferencing, which has a certain sex appeal or cachet about it that creates a level of excitement that fax machines or e-mail have never had.

Because of its attributes, most people's vision of videoconferencing is that its quality should be akin to broadcast television. That is probably not going to be the case—at least for a number of years.

We know of a company in Australia that rolled out its videoconferencing system with such fanfare it could not possibly meet the high expectations that were set. After the first few feeble attempts at using it, the multimillion dollar system lies dormant—a clear case of unreasonable expectations.

Most of our clients who have VC capacity have told us of another type of expectation that must be managed. When they first introduce videoconference systems, their staff will claim they need round-the-clock VC capacity. Staff members do not want to share videoconferencing service. They want dedicated capacity—even if they rarely use it. After all, who wants to share a telephone line? The same is true with video. Without managing these expectations, people may not use your expensive videoconference system.

Unlimited VC capacity is a prestige possession. Our clients say, "Let's videoconference. You do have the capacity, don't you?" They are not really asking a question, but looking for a potential victory in a game of one-upmanship.

9

Interesting Agendas

If the view never changes, watching a monitor can quickly become boring. Unfortunately, this occurs in many videoconference meetings. People do not understand that virtual meetings are not nearly as compelling as in-person meetings. The most frequent complaint we hear about virtual meetings is "Borrrring!" Because of boredom, when participants are off-camera, there is a good chance they are multi-tasking—both watching and working on something else.

Business videoconferences are not like television, where images change about every seven seconds and splashy graphics are flashed on the screen to grab attention. Television producers do this because they know that viewer attention easily wanders, creating the itch to change channels.

Boredom will occur in your videoconference meetings unless you keep everyone focused. Here are some suggestions.

- Set a clear and interesting agenda with frequent changes. When available, use more than one camera so images can shift. When conducting a multisite videoconference, if possible, keep switching from one site to another.

- Do not let any one person speak for too long. Five to seven minutes is optimal.

- Keep referring back to your agenda to focus people's attention.

- Shift the medium so people can do more than watch a video monitor. For example, go off-line to discuss a topic or brainstorm.

- Consider using graphics or an electronic white board to highlight major points.

- Prepare a "storyboard" for best control of your meeting (explained in appendix A). Software packages are available to help you organize your meetings and look your best. Smart Meeting

Pro (available through Oliver World Class Labs) will take you through all the steps of setting up a virtual meeting, let you know who is present at the meeting, and tell you where everyone is located. The software will store electronic documents you want your participants to read before the meeting. It will also generate meeting notes immediately after your meeting is over.

YOUR FIFTEEN MINUTES OF FAME

A certain Nobel laureate and quantum physicist participated in a videoconference that was broadcast to numerous sites.

He treated his audience like a group of students. He scribbled indecipherable notes on a white board. He mumbled. He was dressed as if he were ready to sit down in front of a fire with a book and a cup of tea on a cold winter's night rather than make a public presentation.

This particular videoconference was not the first time he had presented in this fashion. But this was a videoconference that had a huge audience.

In his presentation, he showed little respect for his audience. He seemed to make up his remarks as he went along, flipping back and forth among his points as a new thought struck him. He has since become, as some in his field have described him, a "laughingstock," and not just because he is willing to explore unusual ideas within science.

This antiestablishment attitude that he arrogantly displayed looked particularly bad on video. An academic environment better tolerates brilliant but eccentric professors who can get away with just about anything. Video, however, is more conventional. Well-dressed and well-spoken speakers definitely look the best. Do not waste your fifteen minutes of fame behaving in a way that is appropriate for a very different type of environment simply because that is what you are used to doing.

10

Setting Personal Agendas

Before every videoconference, set an agenda for yourself. As a former executive with Ameritech advised us, "Leverage your time carefully when in a videoconference."[18] Set your own goals whether you are the initiator of the meeting or not. What do you want to accomplish? Would it be useful for you to be in control of the camera console?

Other success-oriented people who are participating in the videoconference with you will undoubtedly have their own personal goals. Without your own goals, you create a vacuum that will allow others to dominate the session.

Make a list of the three to five tasks you want to accomplish as a result of the videoconference. Make sure your list includes at least some items that are specifically related to the medium of videoconferencing and could not be accomplished through e-mail or the telephone. For example, making a strong visual impression on your team at another location is a reasonable goal that is related specifically to videoconferencing. Putting names to faces is another.

Prioritize your list of five goals. If you could only cover four of your goals, which one goal would you eliminate? If you could only cover three, which two would you eliminate?

Attempt to get your highest priority objectives covered early in the conference. It is possible that the system will go down midstream or the meeting will suddenly be terminated for any one of a number of reasons. In this way, you will at least get your highest priorities accomplished.

Matthew, fresh out of an Ivy League college, had an anxious feeling that he was not adequately prepared. But most of his colleagues did not do anything to get ready for the monthly videoconference at the cutting-edge biotechnology firm where Matthew had recently been hired. They just showed up. At least that is what Matthew understood. So that is what he did as well.

Speaking from a remote site, the vice president (VP) of marketing made his initial remarks. Then he started posing specific questions to his project team members who were scattered around the country but now connected on video.

Matthew thought it remarkable how the others who said they did not prepare, knew precisely what to say. When his turn to be questioned arose, Matthew lacked vital information. He could not answer several specific questions the VP asked him. And this was Matthew's first interaction with a senior executive in his organization!

Later, someone asked him why he had not prepared. Matthew was only then told that whenever the VP was on the agenda, team members worked a long night the evening before, making sure they could answer every conceivable question the VP might put to them. Matthew did not know the unwritten rules.

"How was I to know?" he asked. The answer is, you ask. The lesson: videoconferencing is too powerful and visible for you to run the risk of muffing opportunities that it presents to you. You need to be better prepared for this medium than any other.

11

Getting a Great Start

Think of the beginning of your videoconference as if it were a person-to-person meeting—but with greater demands. When you first walk into a VC studio, your remote site or sites may have already called in, and you will be on camera. This can be clumsy because you cannot shake hands as you would in person. One group has attempted to ease this problem by playing music at the main site until people are seated and the meeting is scheduled to begin. Then people start to greet each other at distant locations.

Here are some ways to get a videoconference off to a great start:

- Wave hello. This is becoming a traditional way to start a video-conference. Tell the people at your remote site they look great on your monitor. Most people are a little nervous about their appearance, and they do not know what you are seeing.

- Begin with a well-thought-out introduction, words that capture the essence of your virtual meeting. Remember, people watching television channel surf when a program does not grab their attention immediately. This same itch exists in videoconferences as well.

- Make sure everyone is introduced—especially people who are actively participating in the conference. Even if this takes a little time shifting from one location to another, introductions enhance the feeling of personal connection during a virtual meeting.

- If you are conducting a one-way transmission, greet all the distant sites. Think about how you would start a speech in front of a group of people. You would want to recognize those who are present.

- Introduce anyone who is offscreen. This will prevent the embarrassing situation of someone talking about a person who is in the room but not visible on camera. Acknowledge any observers. If they are ever visible on the screen and you have not introduced them, viewers will wonder who they are.

- If the system you are using has a switcher, you can import the names or titles of participants onto the viewing monitors. In this way, while people are saying hello, their names and titles can be presented. That will save you time and avoid confusion.

- Spell out your agenda. Suggest a time frame for your meeting.

- Lay out the ground rules for the meeting and indicate that unless there are objections, you assume people will follow them.

THE FIRST FOUR MINUTES

Former Reform Party presidential candidate Ross Perot had built up his running mate. He maintained that James Stockdale would defeat the other two 1992 vice presidential candidates in their nationally televised debate—with one hand tied behind his back.

Apparently Stockdale did not get that message. His opening remarks were two self-deprecating questions: "Who am I?" and "Why am I here?"

Unfortunately, the questions did not create a strong introduction. He spent the rest of the evening attempting to recover from one of the weakest openings ever. Those questions have become almost as famous as actor Sally Field's statement when she won a repeat Oscar: "You like me. You like me. You really like me." She, like Stockdale, has lived with those lines ever since. In fact, she recently starred in a commercial where she mocked herself by using those very comments.

As Stockdale so poignantly commented years after the fiasco, "I don't think anyone saw me." Maybe the public did not see the "real" war hero James Stockdale, but they certainly did see an image of him—a very unflattering one.

Making a poor first and lasting impression is the danger of video. Videoconference users are wise to heed Stockdale's lament.

12

Moderators

Moderators can make a multisite or heavily attended two-way video-conference enjoyable—even funny. They can set a tone and establish a theme. On the other hand, if they only enforce rules, they can create boredom. Nonetheless, a moderator must work from guidelines. Here are a few suggestions:

- The moderator's most important role in videoconferencing is telling the group about the protocols in effect and then *nicely* getting people to follow them. Nothing ruins a cooperative videoconference faster than having a dictator for a moderator.

- It is best if the moderator is not the most senior person in the group or the person who called the meeting. An impartial, alert, and sensitive moderator who adheres to the ground rules is preferred.

- Moderators should be technologically savvy about the equipment that is being used. They must be able to recognize where input is coming from if several locations are taking part in the videoconference. One easy way to manage this is to ask the speakers at each site to place a tent card with their site listed. In this way, every time the camera switches to a different location, everyone, including the moderator, will be able to instantly tell where the speaker is from.

- Moderators must also have some degree of emotional sophistication. They are not just managing the equipment—they are allowing people to speak using that equipment.

The moderator should spell out ground rules at the beginning of the videoconference. These should cover topics such as

- The length of time each person will be allowed to speak

- The use of mute buttons

- The length and timing of breaks

- How people will be recognized to speak

It was clear from the beginning of the virtual meeting that no moderator was present. No one was in charge of making sure the videoconference went smoothly for this major technology company.

After a warm-up speech (which was not broadcast to the off-site locations), two panel discussions were scheduled for transmission. The panel discussions proceeded smoothly enough, though they were dominated by two people. These long-winded panelists spoke so long past their allotted time that no one else had an opportunity to ask questions.

Finally, an excited senior executive introduced the closing speaker of the morning. A lot of money had been paid to hire this speaker, an industry expert, and he was being broadcast to six locations around the United States. His message was to be the key event of the videoconference.

Unbelievably, no more than five minutes into this closing presentation, someone in the audience arose stood on his chair, and shouted: "I want attention. I want a standing ovation—now!" The audience cheered the interrupter and gave him what he wanted. Another five minutes went by and someone else stood up and shouted the same request. How did this happen?

The first speaker of the morning, whose speech was not broadcast to the off-site location, had introduced that technique in a very motivational speech and encouraged the audience members to use it whenever they wanted attention. The idea sounded very exciting in his presentation; it, however, ruined the last speaker's presentation and it was broadcast across the United States.

A moderator could have nipped these disruptive outbreaks in the bud. Too bad there wasn't one.

13

Question Handling

The best-phrased answer may be meaningless if everyone has not heard the question. The person who answers a question has obviously heard it, but that does not mean everyone has, especially in a multisite videoconference.

Repeat questions that are posed, unless you are absolutely certain that everyone can hear them. In an international videoconference, repeating questions can be particularly important because of the difficulty in understanding accents and translations.

If you are receiving questions on a computer screen, sent through e-mail, have a person assigned to gather them, group the related ones, and eliminate duplicates. (There will be duplicates, depending upon the size of your audience.)

If you display the e-mails on the screen, have someone clean up spelling mistakes. The person posing the question is probably writing in great haste and would be mortified to see his or her glaring errors projected around the world.

When someone poses a question in a hostile manner, the best way to handle it is simply to repeat the question, minus the hostility— and without any comment. If possible, approach hostile questioners during your next break and remind them that their behavior is being broadcast around the organization and no doubt everyone is now discussing it.

Some questions are not questions. They are statements of long and involved opinion. Larry King has a habit of rudely interrupting his callers in a demanding tone of voice asking, "What's your question? Let's hear your question." That is unnecessary and may inhibit further questions.

Sometimes questions are veiled attacks. Other times, the attacks are not even veiled. A good moderator knows how to deal with these situations. Excellent moderators can reframe an attack disguised as a question so it becomes a reasonable and interesting question.

Here are some examples of questions successfully reframed by a skilled moderator, who delivered the changed question without so much as raising an eyebrow.

- "Why don't you guys ever do your research before you undertake operations like this?"
  Reframed: "The question is, what research was conducted before we started this project?"

- "Who hired that consulting group, in any case?"
  Reframed: "We have been asked to explain our history with our current consultants."

- "We've started so many efforts like this, I can't even begin to count them. When are we ever going to *do* something?"
  Reframed: "The question is, what will be our first implementation steps?"

14

Importance of Participation

Without participation, you run the risk of your off-site video viewers watching something so dull that they will stop paying attention.

On-site audiences will more easily maintain their attention because they are watching a live event, not a broadcast. The off-site viewers are the ones on whom to focus the following tips.

- *Give people a task.* Prearrange comment sessions from off-site groups after a presentation or panel discussion.

- *Use breakout sessions.* Ask participants at each location to go off-line for discussion or brainstorming sessions that will be reported back to the entire multipoint conference. Make sure group leaders are assigned for these breakout sessions.

- *Ask questions before you start.* Pose short, relatively simple, questions to everyone in advance of the meeting. Use these questions—randomly posed to conference participants—at various times during your conference to get input from off-site groups. For example, ask what's the biggest challenge you are facing in your local market today?

- *Prime the pump.* If you ask for feedback or questions from an off-site group that you know is wary of responding on video, arrange in advance with someone from that site to be the first to speak.

- *Take e-mail questions and comments.* Many participants in major VC events are sitting in front of their computers. Make it possible for them to electronically send in their questions. If you do not have time to answer all of them during your videoconference, let people know you will do so after the conference. And make sure you do!

GLASSY-EYED

A few years ago, a well-known Australian news anchor hosted a major internal videoconference for a large multinational electronics company. The subject matter was more than a little technical. Two of the senior participants became completely engrossed in their discussion, challenging each other on the specifications of data interface standards. The camera was locked on the two protagonists.

Twenty long minutes later, one of the participants turned to the news anchor and asked him to make a comment. When a picture of the news anchor flashed on the screen, he was seen slumped in his chair, sound asleep with his mouth hanging open.

A similar situation happened to a second Australian company that organized a multisite videoconference. The moderator was located at a distant site. When the camera flashed to him, he too was sound asleep. No one could awaken him. Someone had to call the off-site location and ask for someone to go into the studio to wake up the moderator.

Incidents like this are embarrassing for everyone. Besides, if the moderators fell asleep during these videoconferences, imagine how many remote viewers also napped through the proceedings.

15

Watching Your Time

Everything takes longer in a videoconference. On many occasions, participants do not understand until they are in the thick of their conference that communication moves more slowly than when meeting face-to-face.

The spontaneity of a quick remark from one person to another sitting across the table is very difficult to duplicate in a videoconference. Not only is spontaneity lost, but the timing required to communicate naturally is compromised. Because of the lack of spontaneity and the slower conversation speed, boredom is also more likely.

Because communication will take longer, be careful with your timing. If you are to deliver a report or make a presentation, find out how much time you have. Then cut your remarks in half. And then cut them again. They will still probably take you twice as long as you anticipate.

Be scrupulous about sticking to the allotted time. Use a time keeper if you need to, and make sure everyone understands the time signals. This is particularly important if participants are using VC systems that may be scheduled for someone else's meeting later.

The rule that news anchors follow is best: three words on paper take one second to speak. Using this formula, you can easily tell how much time your ideas or information will take to present. Most double-spaced pages have approximately 250 words. This means reading a page straight through with no side comments should take you approximately eighty-three seconds. Experiment with this formula yourself.

Some videoconference meetings start late and others go on long after they should end. Here is a list of strategies for starting and ending on time.

- Schedule your meetings to begin at times other than on the hour or half hour. If a meeting is scheduled at 11:03 or even 11:15, more people will be there when you start. We have seen one location call into another with no one in the studio because the participants were all late!
- Do not hold your videoconference at the very beginning of the day. You run the risk that traffic jams will cause people to be late.
- Put your most important agenda items first. And do not review items for people who sign in late.
- If people are habitually late for your virtual conferences, call them personally to encourage them to arrive on time.
- Find out if technical problems are causing the late connections.
- Get administrative assistants to assist you with scheduling and having their bosses sign in on time.
- Discuss the timing problem with members of your group, especially for regularly scheduled videoconference meetings. Ask them how to handle the issue. Let them know how costly their tardiness is.
- Keep your agenda short; know in advance what needs to be covered via videoconference and what can be done through other means.
- Finish on time, even if everything has not been covered. This will send a loud, clear message that will carry over to your next meeting.
- Know in advance which items can be cut when you run short of time. Time definitely will run out, so be prepared.
- Keep reminding everyone where you are on the agenda and how much time remains.
- If all else fails, experiment with a timed agenda, where exact times are listed for each item.

16

International Videoconferences

It is easy to offend someone from your own cultural group—when you intend to offend. It is even easier to offend someone outside your cultural group—without ever knowing you did so. Here are some ways to avoid this problem.

- Acknowledge and thank the people who are most challenged by your worldwide link—those who are up exceptionally early, for example, or those who have stayed at the office exceptionally late. When a meeting occurs outside of normal work hours, apologize for pulling people away from their families and friends. It is particularly critical for corporate officers to thank people as they are normally seen as being able to snap their fingers and get what they want.

- Allocate more time for your international videoconference meetings than for those with your own cultural group. If you know your international colleagues only through videoconferencing, you do not have the benefit of knowing their personal history. Without these personal connections, it is more difficult to smooth over any rough edges in your communication. Discussions will simply take longer.

- If you are using translation services, allocate even more time. Because you are translating across cultures as well as languages, expect that *everything* may take longer. Many Americans, for example, want to come to decisions quickly. A lot of the world finds that idea difficult and even offensive.

- Many around the world also think Americans tend to get too friendly too fast. Determine how close you can get without being offensive—before your videoconference begins. Find out how people want to be addressed: by the use of titles, for example, or by surnames. In other words, pace your international associates.

- Keep reminding yourself that VC technology allows you to span distance; it does not span cultures.

CULTURE COMES THROUGH
DRAMATICALLY ON VIDEO

One American businessman has a strong habit of making the "okay" symbol with his hand (the thumb and forefinger forming the letter O) whenever he agrees with something. When he is on the telephone, this habit doesn't matter. However, in many parts of the world, that gesture is a rude one, in fact, among the rudest.

This particular businessman developed a strong, supportive relationship over the telephone with one of his Brazilian female colleagues. They made a great team, she sourcing manufacturers and he defining product requirements and quality standards.

Then this distribution company got a videoconferencing system.

Now the woman could see her colleague's habitual "nasty" gestures. Because of her unwillingness to say what was upsetting her, it took quite a while to sort out their subsequent miscommunication. The problem slowed down a project the two were working on, and to this day they don't feel as good about each other as they once did.

17

Strong Closings

While the advice we have to offer here is reminiscent of the closing advice we would give any meeting planner, some differences for videoconferences are useful to highlight.

- If you have a moderator, that person will generally make the summary. One way to keep interest in your virtual meeting high—right up to the end—is to announce at the beginning of your meeting that you are going to ask someone for a summary at its conclusion. All participants will take good notes and will also pay attention to whoever is selected to summarize. They will want to compare their own summaries with whoever is chosen to speak for the group.

- The summary should include answers to these questions: What are we going to do? Who will do it? What are the next steps? What are the deadlines? How will we communicate these tasks to each other? When will we meet again? Keep in mind that if the summary involves several people, it will take more time.

- Thank everyone—especially those who have gotten up early or are staying up late—for both their attendance and participation. Tell them you are looking forward to "seeing" them again in your next videoconference. Then wave good-bye—the gesture is becoming standard in virtual meetings. On the telephone both parties say good-bye and hang up, thereby ending the connection. That doesn't necessarily happen in a videoconference. After you have said good-bye, simply get up and leave. There is no need to stare blankly at each other, nervously waiting for the equipment to disconnect.

- Make sure you end on time. If you are in a VC studio, a group of people may be waiting to set up for their own video meeting. Other sites may be using portable rollabout systems that have been scheduled by other people.

"FRANKLY, MY DEAR, I DON'T GIVE A DAMN"

Everything was in place for a prestigious financial institution's multi-site videoconference. The meeting opened with an overview by the moderator. An excellent panel delineated the issues that the group needed to consider. The distant locations seemed to be integrated into the virtual meeting. An appropriate process was even selected for identifying the challenges and solutions the multisite group faced. Unfortunately, not enough time was allocated to finish the sharing after the breakout groups did their work.

The facilitator of the process had to be at another event. He left abruptly at 11:45 A.M. The moderator, who was part of the group, could have picked up the process and completed it for the facilitator, but lunch was waiting outside, and we all know how important it is to eat lunch exactly when it arrives.

One man leaving the room, used the memorable closing words from *Gone with the Wind,* to summarize how he felt. "Why do we do these things if they go nowhere? Especially when we pay all this money to involve our international teams. Maybe they just want to show off our new videoconferencing equipment. I guess it's just more of 'Frankly, my dear, I don't give a damn.'"

18

Following Up

As with any type of meeting, follow-up activity— implementation—must take place to validate your videoconference. Here are some ideas.

- Follow-up demands that you take notes during the videoconference. If you are meeting via the Internet, a document can be created to serve as notes for everyone to see. In fact, people from multiple sites can make corrections to the notes as they are being made.

- If you have questions or receive questions that would break the flow of the videoconference, make a note of them and then ask or answer them after the meeting.

- Advise any remote sites to hold discussions immediately following the meeting—while they are still together. They can summarize the meeting, make sure everyone is in agreement, and create action plans for those items for which they have responsibility.

- Thank people after the meeting. A flurry of e-mails and telephone conversations should be exchanged after a videoconference to acknowledge people. This is especially true after a videoconference with multiple sites and several people. The person-to-person contact will give you an opportunity to say what you perhaps could not say in front of the group.

- If nothing else, an e-mail stating how effective someone was in a conference adds an extra human touch to a situation that may have been uncomfortable for some.

One of the biggest problems with meetings, whether the meeting is in person or a videoconference, is that people do not follow through.

People who are effective users of videoconferences are usually meticulous about sending summary memos after their meetings. And they put their names on them. Senior executives tell us this is the best way to ensure people do what they have agreed or were assigned to do. Here is their advice:

- Put your most important messages in the first and last paragraphs. Those are what people tend to read.

- Write a summary of your meeting in the first paragraph. Emphasize the medium of videoconferencing. Liberally sprinkle phrases such as "we saw," and "as everyone could see" throughout your summary.

- Put action items in the last paragraph.

- Put details in the middle paragraphs. People who like details will read them.

- Do not worry about winning the National Book Award with your summary. Accuracy and speed are the most important attributes to ensure follow-through after your videoconference.

- Create "breathing space" in your memo. That is, use wide margins and space between the paragraphs.

- Use headings and bullets to make reading easier.

- Keep the memo simple. Avoid big words, complicated phrases, or strange acronyms that some may not know.

- Use personal pronouns. Say, "We decided" instead of "It was decided."

- Always thank people for participating. Tell them you were "glad to see them."

19

Lessons Learned

We recommend a simple "lessons learned" evaluation be conducted after every videoconference in which you participate—at least until you get to the point where you feel you no longer are learning anything new.

Even if you are an old pro at videoconferences, if you meet with a group of people who have varying degrees of virtual experience, conduct a "lessons learned" evaluation to enhance the learning experience for people who are new to videoconferencing. When videoconferences go well, people who lack experience will have no idea what ingredients, habits, or behaviors made their meeting a success. If you want newcomers to this technology to be able to transfer this knowledge to their own videoconferences, they need to have the successes underscored.

Here are three simple questions that will cut to the heart of "lessons learned."

- What went well?

- What could have been handled or done better?

- What lessons did we learn that we can take to our next videoconference meeting?

DON'T GIVE UP YOUR POWER TO THE TECHNICIANS

Having technical assistance available can create a situation where nontechnical people stop thinking about the fundamentals of what they want to accomplish in their videoconferences. Remember, however, that from the participants' point of view, presenters are responsible for their virtual meetings.

Janelle was the sole presenter in a six-hour live conference in Ljubljana, Slovenia, that was transmitted via ISDN lines to Skopia, Macedonia, about a thousand miles away. Both audiences of approximately one hundred participants each had some members who used translators. Janelle worked with PowerPoint, played music, and involved both sites in activities. The elaborate production took place without major problems.

When Janelle asked herself at the conclusion of the meeting what she learned, she knew immediately. "Don't give up your power to the technicians."

During a dry run of the program held the day before the conference, every attempt was made to get Janelle's Macintosh Titanium G4 to run with the VC equipment. That was not possible, and all attention was focused on how to solve that problem. The equipment was already in place; all the lines were firmly adhered to the floor with duct tape. When testing the equipment, everyone faced the camera and monitor that was positioned on the stage to the right of Janelle. Janelle's audience was to be in front of her.

It was not until ten minutes prior to the start time that Janelle realized the camera and monitor needed to be on the floor facing her—giving people at the remote site a feeling of being talked to instead of receiving a constant side view. Unfortunately, it was too late to make changes. Janelle recognizes that she did not thoroughly think matters through—primarily because of the abundance of technical help. She will not make that mistake again!

PART 4

HABIT 3
Make Technology Your Friend

THE BIG PREMISE: EQUIPMENT IS UNFORGIVING

Many people think that the biggest problem with VC technology is frequent equipment breakdowns. That certainly is an issue.

But an even bigger issue than breakdowns is what happens when the VC equipment operates perfectly. It is extremely unforgiving.

If you do something to VC equipment, it does something in return. When working with a voice-activated camera, for example, if you have not muted your microphone, the camera will expose you on the monitor the moment you blow your nose. When you thump on a microphone, it will register that sound. If you retract your ballpoint pen within twenty-five feet of a microphone, nonlocal sites will clearly hear the click. If you wear inappropriate patterns or colors, they will glare or vibrate under a camera lens. Unless you are using three-dimensional VC, an object on the wall behind your head will appear to sit on your head. We saw a speaker with a Buddha "growing" out of his head—the statue was in a display case behind him. Finally, if you are being recorded, your words and your expressions will be captured for posterity.

Marshall McLuhan, Canadian sociologist, penned the well-known expression "the medium is the message." In other words, the content of any form of communication is influenced by the medium of communication used. The same message will come across differently by e-mail, telephone, fax—or in a videoconference.

For example, people have lower expectations for e-mail than for videoconferences because the benchmark for e-mail is a quickly jotted note. As a result, we are more forgiving about errors in e-mails. Videoconferencing is benchmarked against the medium of broadcast television. Videoconferencing, therefore, demands a different level of awareness. It is not necessarily more intimate or capable of replacing other types of communication. But it introduces information in a way that says, "Respect me, or you'll pay a price."

20

Microphones

Microphones come in all shapes and sizes. Some are desk or podium mounted, others are on a boom, and yet others are connected to lapels. Many VC microphones are built into the camera itself so you do not have to worry about them at all.

Do not be fooled into thinking a smaller microphone means less volume. Today's microphones are more sensitive than ever. Many are multidirectional and will pick up the softest whisper or background noise. They can be set so the various voice strengths of everyone seated at a table will project at the same volume.

Finally, because of the transmission delay that occurs when people speak from different locations, help your remote site participants know when it is their turn to speak by using such phrases as, "I'll end here." This is basic VC etiquette and when used periodically will make your site exchanges smoother.

Here are some tips to help you master using a microphone:

- Test whether your microphone is working by scratching the surface gently. Do not bang on it and never blow into it.

- Notice background noise and reduce it. Even the sound of shuffling paper is noisier than you realize in a videoconference. The clicking sound of a ballpoint pen being retracted is also more noticeable.

- Echoes can easily occur near any hard surfaces. To minimize them, place curtains over the windows, remove pictures from the walls, and cover the floor with carpet.

- Do not lean too close to the microphone or your *p*s will pop and your *s*s will sound like hisses.

- Definitely speak in a normal tone of voice. Many people sound as if they are shouting when they use a microphone.

- If you wear a lapel mike, never thump on your chest. Prevent jewelry from touching the mike, and never wear your microphone into the bathroom!

- To create a smooth line with a wireless mike, run the cord through your clothing and out the bottom of your shirt. Clip the battery pack to the rear of your clothing.

- If you are on a panel or at a remote site, mute your microphone until you speak. If not, any inadvertent noises (including conversations with someone else as well as inadvertent burping, coughing, sneezing, swallowing, or swearing) may suddenly be transmitted for everyone to hear.

THE WORLD IS LISTENING

Even the pros can get it wrong. Most actors work with boom microphones and have had little experience with desk- stand-, or podium-mounted mikes or lapel mikes.

As a result, you will see many movie and television actors lean into microphones when being interviewed on chat shows or when they are on stage.

During the 2001 Emmy Awards, for example, Jennifer Garner, lead actor in one of the season's new television shows, *Alias,* leaned into the microphone, attacking it as if she were eating an ice cream cone.

Not only was it unattractive to see her hunched over and attempting to consume the mike, that posture distorted her voice. And it was completely unnecessary.

Knowing the power of your equipment is very important. She should have asked. And so should you.

21

Cameras

Many people are afraid of video cameras despite the smallness of today's portable cameras. People feel exposed and vulnerable looking into that black lens. If you are interviewed on a television show, the host will tell you to talk with him or her and not look into the camera. That rule, however, does not apply to videoconferences. You are trying to replicate the feeling of an in-person meeting with distant sites, so looking into the camera is important.

The camera can be your friend if you follow a few simple tips:

- Know where the camera is.

- Some cameras can focus well enough to clearly read and transmit the serial numbers on a dollar bill, but that does not mean those at the receiving end can read a piece of paper you hold up to the camera. It is best to use a document camera when displaying documents.

- When working with a voice-activated camera, a slight delay can occur while the camera locates who is speaking, particularly if the room is crowded. As you wait for the camera to capture your image, consider using filler phrases such as, "Speaking from New York" or "I'd like to emphasize one point."

- Think through the impact of your videoconference before it begins. Most of the time, it is best to look into the camera. If a larger audience is assembled at your local site, however, it may be more appropriate to look at your local audience.

- After you finish speaking, pause and look into the camera lens for a second or two. This will give your message greater authority and ensure smoother transitions to graphics, other locations or the next speaker.

- So you do not leave the camera's view when delivering a presentation on your feet, mark your "on-camera zone" with masking tape on the floor.

- Never watch yourself on the monitor. Nothing will make you lose your credibility faster and make you look like a rank amateur. Look at other people around you or at the camera—the other "person" in the room!

"LOOK MOM, I'M ON TELEVISION"

The next time you have an opportunity, watch a big sporting event on television. Notice the audience reaction to the television cameras.

Most people are sophisticated enough to know that when that red-lighted television camera is pointed at them, they are being transmitted across the ether to a huge home audience. What an opportunity!

Naturally, they want to see themselves as the home viewing audience will see them. So, they turn to the gigantic screens that most sports arenas display all over the stadium to catch the live feed. They—and the viewing audience at home—see a nice side view as all the heads turn. Too bad no one has invented a monitor that we can simultaneously look at and simultaneously see ourselves head-on.

Besides not looking at the monitor, here is one more tip. If you have a desk videoconferencing unit with the camera placed on top of your computer, the camera will be positioned above your head. Though the camera can be angled, the nonlocal site might see a picture that emphasizes the top of your head when you are looking at your computer screen (though the good news is that it will reduce the size of any double-chins you might have). The solution is to push yourself out from your desk a little way so you can look more directly into the camera. Angle the camera to point down as much as possible. You can also sit on something to make you taller or adjust the height of your chair. If your computer keyboard is mounted on a pullout tray, that extra distance will also help to give you a more direct face shot.

22

TelePrompTers

TelePrompTers—off-camera devices that allow a presenter to see a magnified script—are commonly used today for important speeches that are beamed to distant locations. The advantage of using modern TelePrompTers is that they are situated so you can read from them and still look as if you are peering directly into the camera lens. You give the impression of knowing what you are talking about, sound more fluent, and can speak at great length without consulting notes.

The newest models are voice activated and stay ahead of the speaker. Some models even display the text of the speech directly on the camera lens itself. Whatever type you have available, TelePrompTers do take some getting used to.

Normally TelePrompTers display four words per line and include three lines ahead of where you are speaking. The lines move at the speed of your voice. If you slow down, so will the TelePrompTer. If you rush ahead, fearful that the words will pass you by, the TelePrompTer will just speed up to accommodate you.

If you will be using a TelePrompTer, be sure to practice with one until you feel comfortable with the technology. Fortunately, the learning curve is very quick.

However, unless you practice first, your inexperience will show when you are speaking. Your eyes will move from left to right as if you are watching a tennis match. Get your feet wet first—without an audience!

IMPRESSIVE!

Any technology can go wrong, and it is best to be prepared for disaster.

In 1999, U.S. President Bill Clinton—a master of video—was set to give his annual State of the Union address to Congress, the people of the United States, and the world.

As soon as Clinton started his speech, he realized that the technicians had cued his 1998 State of the Union address on the Tele-PrompTer.

Clinton kept right on talking, ad libbing the beginning of his current State of the Union address until a technician figured out what was happening and loaded the correct speech.

No one in the nation or the Congress knew what was happening. That poise was truly presidential. Even Clinton's political enemies were impressed once they found out what happened.

23

Lighting

While everyone seems to know that the camera adds at least ten pounds to your appearance, most people do not know that lighting can make you look like an extra in a horror movie. Here are some ideas to make lighting work to your advantage.

- If there are windows in the room, sit facing the windows. Any camera facing strong window light will cast your face in shadow, eliminating your facial features.

- Avoid backgrounds with large white spaces (walls or doors). Faces should be the lightest color in the view of the camera lens.

- If you are only lighted from the head down (which is how room lights are normally placed), your nose can look enormous, and your jaw will appear to sag. Or you will get double chins, even if you do not have them, and unflattering shadows on your face. Your eyes may look as if you did not get any sleep last night. To solve this problem, experiment with uplighting. Hold a bright white sheet of paper under your chin so you can see how uplighting looks on your monitor. If it makes a difference—and it can make a huge difference—put a lamp on the floor with soft light projected upward.

- If you are light-skinned, avoid a lot of white around your face. A white shirt is fine. However, with too much white in the area the camera lens sees, your image will be too dark to distinguish facial features. If your skin is dark toned, you can wear much brighter, stronger colors. Do not hesitate to adjust the contrast and brightness controls on your camera.

- Before your videoconference session begins, check your image on the monitor. Angle your head to see if unflattering shadows appear on your face.

- Even though most videoconference studios that are available for rent by the hour use normal internal room lights, some studio lighting can be very bright and hot after a few minutes—like staring into bright sunlight. Be prepared to sweat. Wear lightweight clothing and bring tissues to wipe your brow.

- If you have any control over light installation, choose bulbs with a good color balance. Some fluorescent lights cause the skin to look green and sickly.

IS MY NOSE REALLY THAT BIG?

When it comes to lighting problems, we have seen it all:

- Warm yellow lights that made people look as if they were suffering from yellow fever or bad liver function.
- Light so intense that it washed out all the colors on people's clothing and, more importantly, on their faces; they looked half dead.
- Overhead lights that created a merciless glare on all the bald heads in the room.
- Lights so hot that they triggered a very noisy air conditioning system whose loud roar was transmitted around the world.
- Beautiful glass artwork that reflected an unbearable glare.

But the worst lighting problem we have ever seen was lights placed in the ceiling right over a participant who, inarguably, had a good-sized nose to begin with. By the end of the conference at a multinational pharmaceutical company, the size of his nose was the topic of conversation. As cruel as it was, some people in off-site locations began taking bets on just how large his nose was.

Technical people generally do not pay attention to issues like this. They primarily want to make sure the equipment works. It is up to the individuals involved in the videoconference to adjust the lighting to keep their noses down to size.

24

Taping

It is very easy to make a videotape of anything that is being captured by camera and transmitted. Chances are that many videoconferences you take part in will be recorded by somebody, somehow, somewhere. Here are some tips to protect yourself.

- Work from the proposition that there is no such thing as "off the record" in videoconferencing. It is wise to assume that your conference is being saved for posterity, even if it is not.

- People participate in a different way when a tape recorder is being run. If you need a frank, no-holds-barred conversation, do not conduct that conversation in a videoconference.

- Videotapes of conferences are records that can be used in depositions in legal cases. For this reason, organizations should assume all videoconference meetings are public documents and advise their staff of such.

- For yourself, make a clear decision to tape or not to tape. The tape recorder becomes a person in the room with an indelible memory. Do not make the decision lightly.

- You may argue that you can easily delete the record if something inadvertent gets said on it. Destroying a tape also sends a message. Remember President Nixon and his audiotapes. While the world may never know what was on the thirteen minutes deleted from one of Nixon's tapes, everyone assumes it was something that would have implicated him.

Allan Funt, the host of *Candid Camera,* understood that Americans (and perhaps the entire world) love to see people in embarrassing situations. His program started a trend that only will be enhanced with modern videoconferencing.

Television is full of shows about bloopers—sports bloopers (where this term for a public blunder originated), ordinary people's bloopers, and outtakes from television shows and movies. Perhaps CNN or MSNBC will soon offer a show featuring company videoconference bloopers.

When we watch sports bloopers, we rarely focus on the fact that someone probably got hurt in the incident. The same is true with videoconference bloopers. These are not innocent affairs. Someone gets hurt with these tapes. People are forever branded with embarrassing images.

A videotape is available of former vice president Dan Quayle's bloopers. For $14.95, you can watch twenty-five minutes of his convoluted sentences, incorrect facts, and malapropisms, including his comments on the Holocaust:"It was an obscene period in our nation's history. We all lived in this century. I didn't live in this century, but, but in this century's history."

Unfortunately for Quayle, this verbal blooper will live on forever, taped for future generations to see.

25

Documents

Most videoconferences will be enhanced by mixing documents with "talking heads." Here are some guidelines to help your documents look as good as you.

- *Use big type.* Most people sit some distance from the video monitors unless they are working at their computers. Even a document on a thirty-five inch monitor needs large print to be seen from across the room. Use a thirty-six-point font, which is quite easy to read from a distance.

- *Limit the amount of information you put on each "slide."* We recommend no more than five or six lines.

- *Keep it simple.* If you show something formatted in PowerPoint, avoid using all the features available. Excessive use of "wipes" (animated words or graphics that appear on the screen from various angles) and moving fonts that zoom in from the center can be visually problematical when viewed on a VC monitor.

- *Be careful about colors.* The easiest documents to read are those with dark colors on light backgrounds. One way to see how a document will look is to inspect it on your own monitor. Of course, if your remote site does not have equipment as good as yours, people there will not see the same image quality.

- *Make the type easy to read.* Avoid using all CAPITAL LETTERS and italics. Experts say that both slow down reading. For this reason, they make a nice emphasis but never a steady diet.

- *Use standard typefaces.* The best typefaces to use are sans serif, those without "tails" on the letters. Most computers use Arial, Geneva, or Helvetica as default font for HTML (hypertext markup language), which is how many documents will be displayed at your remote sites. It is, therefore, a good idea to use those typefaces yourself to be assured you are seeing what everyone else is seeing.

- *Leave white space in the bottom right-hand corner.* Because this space is traditionally used for identification text on television, leave that area of your documents blank.

TOO MANY "BELLS AND WHISTLES"

The use of PowerPoint can definitely get out of hand. In one video-conference demonstration, the person who made the slide show must have used every trick that PowerPoint allows.

The letters dropped onto the screen, one letter at a time, each accompanied by the sound of a manual typewriter. Sometimes the letters roared onto the screen, one word at a time, accompanied by the sound of screeching tires. And of course the applause sound was heavily used.

Text zoomed in and zoomed out. On one slide, alternate lines came in from the left and right, floated down from the top and rose from the bottom. The words checkerboarded across and down. They peeked from the bottom, top, left, and right. They flashed at all the speeds that PowerPoint allows and stretched in every direction. They even spiraled onto the page, one of the most annoying features of PowerPoint. The backgrounds were dark colors, and the typefaces, with heavy shadows, were in bright lime greens, sparkling yellows, and shining purples.

Worst of all, the person had timed the show so it was on automatic pilot once it began. Some slides were painfully slow in changing; others were too fast.

Because our faces were being projected on a monitor, we controlled our very strong temptation to roll our eyes and loudly sigh.

26

Murphy's Law

Videoconferencing is wonderful when it works. But many hurdles stand in the way of perfection in videoconferencing.

Videoconferencing on personal computers in particular creates problems because of the variety of equipment and software at the receivers' end.

Anticipate that Murphy's Law—if anything can go wrong, it will—will operate in full force during your videoconference. Systems can and will go down. You may have visual contact but no audio. You may have audio contact, but no visual. The system may be down at one end—and no one may know it. The people who are watching may lack sufficient bandwidth to view your Webcast. The audio portion of your Web feed may be faster than the video segment, creating terribly out-of-synch voice and video. Some sites may have firewalls (software that limits access to a network) preventing your transmission from getting through.

When in doubt, reboot! In many—if not most—cases, rebooting the codec (the equipment enabling video and audio to be transmitted) will solve your problem.

You always need a contingency plan if the technology fails. One obvious alternative would be to immediately hook up with a teleconference. Make sure you know everyone's cellular telephone numbers in advance so you can easily communicate if your VC connection is lost. You might want to set a time limit of fifteen minutes to try to reconnect before you give up.

Practice and patience will help. And look for the humor in the situation. Finding it will not solve your problem, but it will help your mood.

IF IT CAN HAPPEN TO JESSE

Minnesota governor Jesse Ventura, speaking from Cambridge, Massachusetts, was being Webcast to multiple locations. The plan was to make Ventura available to answer questions after his speech. The audience could ask questions through their monitors via computer hookups.

Unfortunately, the information technology people could not receive the feed from Cambridge at many of the nonlocal sites. After twenty minutes, most of the audiences left the locations where the transmission was not working. Ventura had a meager audience.

Unfortunately, the speaker is the one who looks bad in a situation like this, even though he or she will not find out about it until after the event is over. Remember, if it can happen to a former professional wrestler turned governor, it can happen to you.

PART 5

HABIT 4
Maximize
Your Presence

THE BIG PREMISE: THINK ABOUT AMPLIFICATION

When people see themselves for the first time on a television screen, most are shocked to discover how much heavier they look. The lens of a camera, as we have previously noted, automatically adds ten pounds—to everyone.

Everything, in fact, gets amplified on video. Therefore, every aspect has to be carefully monitored to maximize your presence. When you are in a large, open room, any single item in the room can be swallowed up by the large space that surrounds it. With videoconferencing, however, camera angles tend to be much tighter, so space is much smaller. As a result, whatever is seen occupies more of the frame and stands out.

Think about amplification as the guiding principle for everything you do while on camera. Perhaps even more unsettling is, as we have emphasized before, if you make a mistake that is being recorded, not only will it be amplified, but it could be available for the world to see over and over again.

In 1998 Bill Gates testified in the trial of the U.S. government against his company Microsoft. Gates normally handles media questions very effectively, but this was interrogation. Under pressure, he seemed insincere, arrogant, and uncaring. And the world got to watch him at his worst—repeatedly on the evening news and endlessly on business television talk shows.

As you strive to use this new technology effectively, be careful not to conclude that videoconferencing is just a different means (less troublesome and less expensive than flying) of meeting with people. It is much more than that. In many ways, VC is bigger than life.

27

No Food, No Gum

Every individual has different beliefs about eating, and you set yourself up to offend someone if you eat while on camera. Even more offensive is trying to talk while you are eating. The best rule to follow is not to do any chewing while participating in a videoconference.

That can be particularly challenging if the videoconference goes on for quite a while. When that happens, take a break if you need to eat.

In some virtual meetings, one site has sandwiches brought in and the other site has nothing to eat. In person, this would be terribly rude. It is not much better on video.

What about beverages? Peter Grace, chairman of the Grace Corporation, once gave us some good advice. We met him at a Bangkok cocktail reception where, naturally, everyone had a glass of wine in his or her hand—except Peter Grace. Television cameras were about, as this was an important group that had gathered. He told us that it doesn't matter what is in the glass—a Coke or water. It will look like you are drinking alcohol. That will offend someone. And to others it sends the wrong message. It looks like you aren't working.

If you want to drink water while in a videoconference, have a glass with a container of water close by. Use clear glass, so it is obvious that you are drinking water. In general, stay away from beverages in containers especially when holding an international videoconference, since many people find drinking straight from a can to be behavior of the lowest class.

AN INTERNATIONAL
FOOD FEST

Janelle tells of her participation in an international conference that was linked to audiences around the world, including Brazil.

At the beginning of the conference, everyone was introduced—about two hundred people in Washington, D.C., several dozen more at distant locations around the world, and two women from Brazil. One of the Brazilians was particularly heavyset.

She entered the room with a bagful of food, which she carefully organized on the table in front of her. Video from each distant site was projected on a gigantic screen for the Washington participants to enjoy. Over the next three hours, we watched her go through every morsel of her banquet.

After a while, one could hear members of the audience in Washington make remarks about the woman. Given the amount she was eating and her size, you can be sure the remarks were not flattering.

28

Distractions

When someone engages in distracting behavior, it often means the person lacks power or status. Children, for example, often behave in a manner that is distracting. Power, on the other hand, is broadcast by firmness and steadiness. Remember, your behavior will be amplified with videoconferencing. Here are some ideas to consider.

- Drinking from coffee cups looks more distracting on video than in person. Smoking definitely does not look good.

- Take note of your chair. Adjust it so you sit up taller. Stay away from swivel chairs. Even slouching can be a distraction, and erect posture will give you maximum presence. Do you think no one can see your legs? If you swing them, the movement will be propelled through your upper body. You will look like a squirming child on too tall a chair.

- When seated on a studio chair similar to a bar stool, put your feet on the crossbar—and do not move your legs. (It is tempting to swing your legs if they are hanging.) If your legs or feet will appear in the video, plant both feet firmly on the floor.

- Some people pick up a strong habit of twirling their pens and pencils like a helicopter and become very adept at it. In person it is highly distracting, and on video the twirling totally focuses the viewer's attention. Put your pen down if you cannot avoid tapping, doodling—or twirling!

- When videoconferencing at your desk computer, clean up your work space so it does not look like piles of paper, left over Coca-Cola cans, and crumpled paper have invaded your life.

- One "distraction" that seems to work well are plants or flowers. Even fake ones can soften your setting and give it a lived-in look and feel.

- Finally, if you react to a distraction that is off-camera (for example, someone opens a door and walks in), let your remote audience know what happened. This will help them feel as if they are in the same room with you.

THE TOUPEE THAT WENT ASTRAY

At one internal videoconference, a dominant person in the group clearly wore a toupee. How did we know? Because the hairpiece was actually askew. It was not only crooked, it came close to touching his eyebrows. It was black in color, and all the gray hairs at the nape of his neck stuck out.

No one felt comfortable telling him about the problem. So the conference started.

People held their breath, waiting for the hairpiece to fall off. Even the cameraman could not avoid fixating on the wig gone awry. Perhaps he did it unconsciously, but that cameraman kept panning over to the man's head, ending up with a close-up focus on the toupee.

We have no idea what the toupee wearer's message was, we were so distracted by his hair problem. We suspect that everyone else in the conference had the same reaction.

Like this poor fellow, the worse your distraction is, the less likely people will tell you about it. You are going to have to notice these problems yourself. Look in a mirror before going into a videoconference or look at yourself on the display monitor before your meeting begins. If you are at your computer for a desktop videoconference, you will not have a display monitor to check, so you will have to scrutinize yourself and your space from the viewer's perspective.

29

Patterns and Colors in Your Clothing

Your eyes do not see the same colors that the monitor displays. Reds are the most dangerous, frequently projecting as brown or orange—not the most flattering colors on most people. Reds also project too brightly and can shimmer. Use red in small amounts. If you want a relatively true projection of the color you are wearing, stick to blues.

While a little bit of white will reflect light on your face, making your eyes appear brighter and giving your face a healthy glow, wear white only as an accent color. White in large amounts is too glaring and will darken your face. White or light blue dress shirts look very professional on men. For more formal videoconferences, leave your suit jacket on.

Women have much greater variety available to them in their clothing choices. Watch female anchors on television whose skin tones match your own to see what would look best on you.

And never forget that the camera adds about ten pounds to your girth. Dark colors (navy, black, charcoal, dark gray or dark brown) will create a slimming effect because dark colors recede. Light colors come forward.

Even if you look great in bright yellow, do not wear it on camera—you will look like a giant canary or large banana. Your face or message will in no way be able to compete.

Neutral, solid clothing is best. Stay away from herringbone patterns, close stripes, plaids, Hawaiian-style floral designs. Any pattern that makes it difficult for the camera to focus will produce a moiré pattern. Moiré patterns (the wavy lines that appear when graphics are shown with inappropriate resolution) create a strobe effect. They are difficult to watch and even give some viewers a headache.

If you are in a conference room with a sky blue or green background (called a chroma key), make sure your clothing color is different from the background. If your clothing and the chroma key are the same, you will "key out." In other words, your head and hands will appear as if floating while your body disappears into the background. This ghostly effect may be interesting at Halloween, but it is devastating in a videoconference.

CNN SHOULD KNOW BETTER

Paula Zahn is a very good on-camera anchor for CNN. But in early October 2001, she was on camera for her entire morning show wearing something most veteran television people never wear—a blouse with a strong herringbone pattern.

The wavy moiré effect was awesome. Paula appeared to bounce all over the screen. CNN has excellent video equipment, yet it could not contain the wavy projection patterns on Paula's blouse. If CNN cannot control them, imagine what she would have looked like on a Webcast or a videoconference with much lower-end equipment. When a computer attempts to connect the pixels or dots that abound with striped or herringbone patterns, they look like twinkly Christmas-tree lights to the viewer.

Paula also wears bright reds that no doubt are stunning in person. On screen, however, the reds create glare for the viewer. If a sophisticated television anchor makes these mistakes, imagine how easy it is for businesspeople to choose inappropriate colors and patterns in their clothing.

Anger and Other Negative Emotions

Anger signifies that something is important. We do not get angry about issues that are unimportant to us. So when we see someone else get angry, we become curious to know exactly what will happen next and our interest level peaks.

When you write an angry e-mail and send it immediately, it is a very quick display of your anger. Anger on video is even more immediately displayed—and amplified. The nonlocal site will no doubt play and replay your message, if recorded, attempting to figure out what you really meant.

Save your anger for after your videoconference or for in-person meetings. While you are on camera, breathe when you feel yourself getting aroused and irritated. Avoid talking when you are angry. If you have a tendency to easily get angry, write yourself a reminder note about not getting angry and place it on the paper you have in front of you. Although surveys note that about 40 percent of people express anger in meetings, it is best avoided in videoconferences.

Like anger, many negative emotions—sarcasm, resistance, arrogance, negativity, gloating, bitterness, distrust, and even indifference and disappointment—come across strongly on camera and are commonly expressed in meetings. They are best avoided in a medium that amplifies them.

Former vice president Al Gore is known as a very good debater. But in 1993, many people thought Reform Party presidential candidate Ross Perot would easily defeat him in the televised debate over NAFTA (the North American Free Trade Agreement). Gore reversed the situation by getting Perot angry; he unnerved Perot by repeatedly interrupting him. Perot was so frazzled that all he could do was focus on the fact that he was being interrupted.

As you read the following sound bite, imagine Perot's pedantic look when he lectured and his nasal twang that intensified when he was annoyed. It did not look pretty.

GORE: How would you change it?

PEROT: Very simply. I would go back and study—first, we should look at this. It doesn't work. If—

GORE: But what specific changes would you make in it?

PEROT: I can't—unless you let me finish, I can't answer your question. Now you ask me, and I'm trying to tell you.

GORE: All right. Well, you brought your charge tonight, so I want to know what specific changes you would like to make in the treaty.

MODERATOR: That's a fair question. If you're against it, let him respond.

PEROT: I—how can I answer if you keep interrupting?

MODERATOR: All right.

GORE: Go ahead. Go ahead. (End of sound bite)

Perot came apart, undone by his own anger. Anger is an emotion for all of us to avoid on video.

31

Assume You're Live

When the system goes down—and it will—assume you are still "live." Just because you cannot see what is going on does not mean that other participants at other sites cannot. Do not even trust your own technicians to be able to tell.

The system can fool people in many ways. They think their microphones are turned off because they have been told the system is down, or that they are experiencing "system trouble." They turn their heads to make what they think is an off-camera remark to a colleague. The remark is off-color, derogatory, or spills information that should not be shared. Everyone else can hear it.

Here is one piece of good advice from salespeople that everyone should carefully apply to this new world of virtual meetings. Salespeople recommend that when visiting a client on a sales or service call, never make any negative remark while in the client's building. You do not know who is in the rest room with you. You do not know who that person in the elevator is or the person walking down the corridor. A security system may be recording your every word and action, and you will never know it.

Follow the same advice at a videoconference. Assume that your equipment is working and recording from the moment you enter a video space. Act as if whatever you say can be heard throughout the system and whatever you do can be seen by others and may be recorded. Modern VC systems generally take a moment to disconnect or "drop" the call at the end of a virtual meeting, so make sure your call is completely disconnected before making remarks that may not be appreciated by viewers at nonlocal sites.

A GURU GOES "LIVE"

One of our absolutely favorite people has been named the world's number one business management guru. But even he has blown it during a videoconference.

This esteemed elder statesman was asked to participate in a video-conference that was being projected to a large group of high-level business executives in Mexico City. He was asked to deliver his remarks to the conference via video from Los Angeles.

Murphy's Law was in full force that morning. The system went down—at least at the guru's end. Unfortunately, the visual feed without sound was projecting clearly to the hotel meeting room in Mexico City.

Participants in Mexico could hear our hero say, "Hello, Mexico." Everyone could also hear a technician tell the presenter, "We aren't getting through yet." Obviously, the guru had no idea that anyone could see him.

He proceeded to pick his nose. As one of the audience members in Mexico City said, "He had his arm in his nose up to his elbow!"

The top level Mexican executives nearly fell out of their chairs laughing at this event. We understand it was the highlight of the morning. Unfortunately, our guru did not have a clue! Always assume you are live, even if you are told you are not!

32

The Importance of Being on Time

A salesperson with a customer who wants to place an order will only keep that customer waiting under the most extreme circumstances. Customers, however, feel quite comfortable making their vendors wait. After all, salespeople generally need the customers more than the customers need them. If you are kept waiting, perhaps you are being sent a message that you are expendable or less important.

Most staff members will not make their bosses wait for them, but managers frequently make their staff wait for them. Patients wait for the doctor; the doctor will not wait for them.

With videoconferencing, however, if you come in late, you will not appear to have more power. If people who called into a videoconference meeting see an empty room, it looks very bad. A multisite videoconference will undoubtedly have started without you, so you will just look rushed if you come in late. Remember the principle of amplification.

Furthermore, if you arrive late and cannot try out the equipment before you start, every mistake you make or mishap that occurs with the equipment—even if it has nothing to do with your late arrival—will be seen as having to do with your tardiness.

Being on time or arriving late both send a message. Most everyone will read a negative unspoken message in tardiness, even if the message was not intended. Also remember that both sides could be paying for the use of the equipment. Your tardiness will cost someone else, who will not appreciate it.

"NO-SHOWS" CAN BE EXPENSIVE

Two legal teams, one on the East Coast of the United States and another on the West Coast, had scheduled their first meeting via a videoconference. Each team was representing a different side in a huge lawsuit.

The East Coast team decided to show the West Coast team that the legal action was not so very important to their client by arriving thirty minutes late to the videoconference studio. They knew it would take another thirty minutes to get everyone ready to meet the West Coast legal team on video, so they were, in effect, a full hour late for the meeting.

By the time they were prepared to be introduced to the West Coast lawyers, they were told that no one was in the studio. The West Coast legal team had decided to cancel the meeting. They left word for the East Coast lawyers that they were sorry some sort of "miscommunication" had occurred—there obviously was a mix-up in the time and date for the videoconference. They also said that they would leave word with the client that the meeting needed to be rescheduled.

When the executives of the organization being sued learned what had happened, they fired their East Coast legal team. They argued that "power posturing" had cost them the opportunity to settle the case before more costly legal action was necessary.

33

When You Are on a Panel or Part of a Group

When a panel participates in a videoconference, the camera is normally positioned so all members of the panel can be seen simultaneously. This position is not only visually uninteresting, it lets everyone at remote sites view every reaction members of the entire panel have to whoever is speaking.

There is a reason why no more than two people are seen sitting at television news desks. Our peripheral vision blurs activity that takes place on the sides of the picture. When television news shows need to show more than two people on camera simultaneously, they seat them around a table or angle them in chairs, rather than arranging them in a straight line facing the camera.

When you are part of a group, point out that if you all sit exactly the same way, you will look artificial, tense, and forced when the camera shows a wide angle. Assume slightly different postures with the people positioned at the ends of the table turned toward each other. The whole group will look better.

Professional speakers give this advice to people appearing on panels:

- Assume that everyone in the room is looking at you—always. Certainly *someone* is! This is in part what makes VC challenging—in many virtual meetings you are never out of camera view. During in-person meetings, the group's attention wanders around the room, giving you a chance to scratch your head, stretch, or adjust your clothing. You do not have that opportunity in a lot of videoconferences.

- Always sit up straight. Lean forward. When you lean back in your chair, you convey either boredom, disagreement, or lack of involvement.

- If you disagree, be careful you do not show that on your face while on a panel. If disagreement registers on your face, you in effect interrupt the other speaker.

- When someone else is speaking, keep an open, friendly, receptive expression on your face—even if you do not feel like it. At least make sure you look neutral if you are feeling negative.

- Take notes. It will help you when you speak and it will also convey an impression of attentiveness.

BOREDOM IS VERY VISIBLE

Lewis Barlow sat in a remote audience with a live video feed of a conference. At various times during the day, a panel would present information.

The panel members paid no attention to their fellow speakers. When it was not their turn, they slumped back in their chairs. They closed their eyes. They all but put their heads down on the table in front of them and went to sleep.

Not only did several hundred people in the audience witness this behavior throughout the day, but thousands of people in remote sites saw it as well.

In the same way, President George H. W. Bush (the elder) got caught displaying boredom and ended up looking old and tired as a result. During one of his debates with then governor Bill Clinton, he glanced at his watch in a way that looked patrician and bored. Who knows what he meant? Viewers only knew how the gesture appeared. And we know he lost the election for a second term as president of the United States.

Displayed boredom is not attractive in video and is strongly amplified. It is best avoided.

34

Makeup

Wearing makeup for the cameras can be a good idea for men as well as women—particularly if the event is an important, broadcasted videoconference meeting. Anyone can sweat under strong or even weak lights. If you do, your face will appear oily to those who are viewing you from distant locations.

People who participate in videoconferences need to keep a little supply of powder in their desk drawers. If male readers find this idea offensive, consider an alternative to powder puffs. Powder can be bought bonded to small pieces of paper bound together in little books. You can take one page and dab your face much the same way you would take a handkerchief and wipe your face. The powder paper will absorb any oil on your face—which is its purpose—and cover any shiny spots. No one will know you are powdering your face.

Bald men in particular have to watch out for this annoying problem, because if their heads are shiny, the bald portion will stand out. This is one reason so many television anchors wear hairpieces. Even though most of us know whose hair is real and whose is a toupee, the hairpiece looks better on television than a shiny bald head.

When on camera, women should wear more makeup than they normally do—but without looking heavily made up. Bright lights diffuse the color on faces. Use dark lipstick colors. If you are going to be in a videoconference meeting that lasts a lengthy period, consider buying the type of lipstick that is semipermanent. The colors do not come off for hours. We have tested them ourselves by blotting our lips on white clothing and the lipstick does not smudge. It's almost magical!

LACK OF MAKEUP CAN COST YOU DEARLY!

Many people believe that Richard Nixon lost the presidency to John F. Kennedy because he lost their first debate. Nixon, as the story goes, refused to wear any makeup. He had seen Hubert Humphrey wear too much makeup in a primary campaign debate against Kennedy in Wisconsin. Nixon believed that Humphrey's makeup is what foiled him—that men did not see Humphrey as manly. Remember, the year was 1960 and most politicians did not understand the medium of television.

Kennedy clearly did. He not only wore professionally applied makeup, but he also took a nap that afternoon so he appeared young, fresh, and vibrant. A large portion of the American public fell in love with him that night.

Nixon did not shave the considerable five o'clock shadow that he sported by the time of the evening debates. In addition, he had been sick a few days earlier and looked dark, pained, and foreboding. The newspapers described him as tense and sweating compared to the unruffled, vital, and in-command Kennedy.

By the second debate, Nixon had learned his lesson, but it was just too late for a correction. Since then, politicians have learned that the image they project often is as important as the substance they represent. Businesspeople need to take their lead and not be squeamish about using makeup when appropriate.

If You Are Sick

If you are sick on the day of a videoconference—even with just a common cold—here are a few "don'ts" to follow.

- If at all possible, do not participate in a videoconference when you are sick. However sick you actually look, you will only appear worse on camera.

- Avoid blowing your nose during a videoconference. Even if you are not speaking, today's sensitive omnidirectional microphones will pick up what most of us consider a socially unacceptable sound from anywhere in the room.

- If you have a cough, consider not talking during the meeting. A cough also gets amplified for everyone to hear. If you absolutely must cough, turn your head away from the microphone and use your hand to direct the sound away from the electronic equipment. Sophisticated studios have a "cough button" on the console. Find out if your system has one and use it.

- Do not loudly suck on cough drops to control your cough. Those slurping sounds can be heard around the world.

- Do not sit in front of a camera if you are feeling nauseous. Those waves of discomfort will definitely show on your face whenever you are on camera.

- Do not take any pills while on camera. You will look like a "pill popper."

- Do not talk about how sick you feel. You will only draw attention to how bad you look.

THINK BUSH-MIYAZAWA

If you are ever tempted to participate in a videoconference while you are sick, think about the time that the senior President George Bush threw up on Japanese prime minister Kiichi Miyazawa's suit.

Bush had begun his trip to Japan by traveling to Australia for a twenty-hour layover. His total trip was twenty-five thousand miles in length, and President Bush was suffering dramatically from jet lag. He was under a tight meeting schedule and attempted to solve his fatigue problems by jogging and playing tennis. His poor stomach did not stand a chance when confronted with some unusual Asian sauces and tastes.

The media was actually very kind to him. The incident was, after all, embarrassing for the entire United States. How many times does one leader of a nation throw up into the lap of another leader? And while being videotaped for the entire world to watch again and again?

Jewelry

When it comes to choosing jewelry for videoconferences, subtle is best. Avoid bright, shining jewelry. Remember the principle of amplification. Jewelry sparkles and catches the viewer's eye. Necklaces and bracelets can bump up against microphones and create a distraction problem.

Some women normally wear many bracelets together as a set. If this is your habit, take them off when you are on camera. You want to look your best, and the bracelets will definitely pull attention away from you.

Earrings should be small. If you choose to wear diamonds, be careful that they are not so large and bright that they flash sparks of light into your viewer's eyes. Even large gold earrings can reflect annoyingly large flashes of light.

Limit the ribbons, tiepins, and badges you wear. Unless you are a decorated military leader, leave the decorations at home.

Men, avoid the "Elvis look" and don't wear gold chains and an open shirt revealing your chest hair.

People who have any visible piercings, other than subtle earrings, should remove the jewelry or studs before the videoconference, if possible. Although tongue studs may seem hidden, many of those who have them tend to stick their tongues out to feel the stud against their teeth. This habit creates a lizard effect and should definitely be avoided.

JEWELRY TALKS

Peta Peter tells the story of an Australian woman who was appointed by the United Nations to an internal position that had previously been held by men only. Needless to say, she was smart and highly respected—and people were watching her closely.

One of her first steps was to introduce herself to all her field offices by means of a videoconference. She wanted to outline her vision for the agency and to describe her strategy for her term in office.

Unfortunately, she broke all the cardinal rules regarding dressing for video. She wore extremely large rhinestone earrings that sparkled and flashed constantly. (At least everyone assumed they were rhinestones. They looked too big to be diamonds.) She also wore a large pendant to match.

Competing with the bright flashes of her jewelry was her white suit jacket adorned with an enormous bucking bronco made of black sequins. It decorated one entire side of her jacket. To accentuate her blue eyes, she wore sparkly blue eye shadow.

The total effect was disastrous. All group discussions focused on her clothing. Nothing was said about her strategy or vision.

She was kept from the public eye for the balance of her term.

Your Voice

Vocal amplification systems are so excellent today you do not need to vocally project—the sound system will do it for you, amplifying all your vocal nuances. If you have external speakers on your computer, chances are you will find that the sound is the best feature of your videoconferences.

Enunciate clearly. This will benefit your conferencing, whether you are video- or teleconferencing. If people regularly ask you to repeat yourself, take it as a clue that you are not enunciating. Do not speak louder, just more clearly.

Here are vocal tips news anchors receive:

- Move your lips so all your syllables can be clearly heard.

- To avoid excessive popping noises (on *p, b,* and *t* sounds), pull your jaw back to sound less explosive.

- *S* and *z* sounds are tricky. To keep from sounding like a cat clawing a blackboard, shorten the duration of your *s* and *z* sounds.

- Voice is more than pitch and projection. It also involves tone, which is as much psychological and physical as it is good technique. Vocal tone is dramatically impacted by how tense you are. To reduce tension, breathe using your diaphragm. The best way to determine if you are doing this is to check for movement in your abdomen. If your stomach extends and contracts as you breathe, you know you are using your diaphragm.

- Make sure you also pronounce your words correctly. In appendix B is a list of commonly mispronounced words. You might be surprised how many people mispronounce commonly used words.

To avoid being stereotyped, many American presidents have moved past their regional accents to project what they hope is a more likeable and seemingly Midwestern presence. It does not happen by accident.

Both Jimmy Carter and Bill Clinton took voice lessons to moderate their southern accents. Ronald Reagan parlayed the skills from his earlier acting career to earn the sobriquet "The Great Communicator." Having stumbled more than a few times, George W. Bush attempts to pronounce his words correctly.

John F. Kennedy, the first media-savvy U.S. president, kept his Scollay Square, Boston accent. He understood Americans thought it sounded sophisticated. His successor, Lyndon Johnson, reveled in his Texas twang, though a lot of Americans found it crude. Businessman and presidential candidate Ross Perot undoubtedly considered his accent a critical part of who he was and never made any attempt to change it—though many grimaced whenever they heard his high-pitched, nasal sounds. The Australian press even nicknamed him "Mickey Mouse" in reference to his voice.

Other American presidents and candidates never successfully projected likability. Richard Nixon somehow always maintained the "bad guy" role. His gruff voice and stiff, jerky movements gave the impression that he thought through everything he did before he did or said it. In large part due to his monotone voice and delivery, Al Gore often appears expressionless. He has paid a price for it.

Whether politicians who shift their vocal presentations to suit audiences lose their authenticity or not is irrelevant. We all play roles, depending on what we attempt to accomplish. If your style interferes with your ability to accomplish your goals, consider making a shift.

Controlling Your Nerves

Before anxiety takes over, try these presenter tips to quell nervousness.

- Visit your videoconference room in advance of your meeting so you become familiar with the room. Comfort with your environment will make you less tense.

- If you are making a presentation during your videoconference, know your material. Rather than memorize your remarks, practice them using key words. You will sound less nervous. Write your key words on a sheet of paper or index cards and place them where you can easily see them.

- If your presentation is very important, you can rehearse in front of a home video camera. You will get immediate feedback as to how you look and will be able to identify your nervous habits. Most people have them.

- Do some unnoticeable relaxation exercises while you wait to speak. For example, with your back straight, breathe in slowly, hold your breath for five seconds, then slowly exhale.

- Look through, rather than at, the lens of the camera. Pretend you are talking to a friendly colleague on the other side of the camera. It will help you connect with your audience and thereby reduce nervous tension.

- Treat the camera like another human being in the room. Visualize this person instead of the camera "eye."

- Be yourself. Do not try to imitate anyone who precedes you. Be as genuine and natural as you are with your colleagues in person during the day.

ROYAL EMOTIONS ARE SHOWING

Prince Charles appears to be almost a caricature of an emotionally remote British royal. His late wife, Diana, was anything but that. As the saying goes, she wore her emotions on her sleeve.

While the public could easily read Diana's moods (which endeared her to the public), it is only possible to spot Prince Charles's tensions through his nervous habits. Granted, the public may not know what the nervous habits are communicating, but they are visible.

Charles picks at his sleeve cuffs. He subtly moves one hand over to his cuff and pulls on it, ever so gently. Then he pulls the opposite cuff. Back and forth he goes, looking like the elegant gentleman that he is, merely straightening his sleeves—though they have not moved since last being straightened.

The habit is telling, particularly if you watch much video coverage of him at all. He is probably not aware of what he is doing. Charles needs to watch himself more on videotape to spot these habits.

So do you. In a recent videoconference, someone we were talking with clasped his hands and placed them firmly on the table in front of him. That gesture was good. Then he began to twirl his thumbs. After the meeting, all four of us in attendance commented on the twirling. Was he nervous? Probably not, but nervousness was what he projected.

Your Eyes

Because we get so much information about others from looking into their eyes, let the camera (your audience) clearly see your eyes. Open them wide. This means no sunglasses—unless you are a rock star and dark glasses are part of your branding. It also means no hat and no long bangs.

Pretend that the camera lens is the other person's eyes, and concentrate on looking *through* the camera. You will create more of a "looked at" feeling for people at the nonlocal site. This is particularly true when you are working at your computer. It is tempting to look at the monitor, since it is typically only about eighteen inches away, rather than at the camera.

How honest you seem is determined by how believable your eyes look. Believability generally means a steady, open, direct gaze and a look that says "I have nothing to hide."

If you can see without your glasses, take them off. If you use reading glasses intermittently, pick them up only when you want to use them. Do not fiddle with or gesture with them.

Notice the way politicians who have attained the age when they can no longer hold a paper out far enough to read keep their glasses in their breast pockets. They take them out for reading and then put them back—looking very astute. Looking out over the tops of half-framed glasses, can make you look like a stern school principal.

Think of glasses as jewelry, and use the same principles for choosing subtle jewelry when deciding which pair of glasses to bring with you. Glasses with heavy frames can make you look severe or angry.

Consider getting nonreflective glass put in your new glasses. Make sure your frames are modern and in style. Large frames look dated. Wire-framed or no-framed glasses are advisable and, if you do lots of videoconferencing, you might want to invest in a pair.

Former U.S. president Bill Clinton was very believable when he came on television and said, "I'm only going to say this once, so listen carefully. I did not ... have sex ... with that woman."

He stared directly into the camera lens. He pointed his finger at Americans. He looked as if he was telling the truth.

Apparently, he had rehearsed his delivery of those lines, and he delivered them well—too well, in this case. He projected the essence of believability—strong voice, strong gestures. But mostly, the effect was in his eyes. He stared into the camera and did not flinch. He was, many of us hoped, letting us into his soul.

Unfortunately, he was only to be believed if you define sex the way that high school students do, as "going all the way." That seemed to stretch the truth as far as most were concerned so it became difficult to believe the president after that.

It's all in the eyes and it's important for all businesspeople who want to be believed to remember this as well.

40

Your Hair

An important rule in television is to get your hair out of your eyes and off your face. While this may be thought of as more of a female issue, many men also have long hair. Public relations (PR) specialists also encourage people on camera to set their hair so it does not move—and PR folk have a lot of experience making people look good.

Constantly moving your hair off your face is a most distracting behavior. People may think it looks sexy to move their hair around, but it annoys the viewer before long. In fact, it can inspire a desire to reach through the lens and cut off the offending hair! If your hair is long (whether you are male or female), tie it back or use hair spray.

Even if your hair does not fall onto your face, keep your hands off your head. It suggests nervousness.

Hair spray is a great product for both men and women to use before going on camera. It keeps hair from moving—especially if a cross current is in the room or you are videotaping outdoors in a wind. If you have an in-house studio, make sure a can of hair spray is stocked in the room. And keep one at your desk just in case you need to bring your hair under control while videoconferencing at your computer.

Remember the principle of amplification. Keep the fine-tuning of your hair private. On camera, you do not want your hair to be a primary distraction.

SOMEONE DOESN'T WANT
TO BE A MILLIONAIRE

Even the unflappable and popular television host Regis Philbin, on *Who Wants to Be a Millionaire,* can get annoyed by hair problems. For example, one contestant looked as if she was going to do quite well until she came to one tricky question—at least, tricky for her.

The more she pondered the question, the more nervous she became. Her long hair fell from behind her ears to cover her face. Every time she leaned forward, down would come her hair. Then she would giggle. Then she would push her long hair behind her ears, using a huge sweeping movement with one hand, fingers spread wide, that started at her brow, went over the top of her head, and somehow ended up with her hair behind her ears. Then she would look up to think. Then down. Then start the sequence all over again.

The first couple of times, the routine was fascinating. By the time the pattern was repeated dozens of times, the contestant had lost everyone's sympathy. Philbin figured out very quickly that this hair routine was not good television. To the audience's relief, Philbin hustled her off the show as soon as possible.

41

Your Clothing

When appearing in a videoconference, simpler clothing is better. Understated, elegant, classic styles are best. Clothing should always look clean and fresh. Your clothing should never be so noticeable that you fade in the background by comparison.

Remember, your head, shoulders, and the upper part of your torso are primarily what is displayed on video. Therefore, avoid clothing that detracts from your face. You should be wearing your clothes—not the other way around.

In a formal meeting, men look best in a dark suit, buttoned, with a white or light blue shirt. For women, a similar style is appropriate, although many women's suits do not require a shirt. Consider adding a neutral scarf. A dark-colored "power suit," with nothing to break up that color, can appear very stern.

If your meeting is very important, check your clothing on a monitor before the videoconference begins. After awhile, you will begin to learn what works for you and what does not.

Many corporations have casual dress days once a week. For important videoconferences, never wear anything less formal than the clothing you would wear on normal work days. Dress even more formally if you are participating in a multisite videoconference; pretend you are going to a distant location to meet with these people. You would probably dress up in person, and so you should on camera.

Keep an extra shirt at the office in case you get called into a videoconference where it is important for you to look your best. Wear garb in which you feel comfortable so you do not find it necessary to smooth your clothing. Any garment that needs attention, is highly patterned, or has frills and ruffles will dominate or invite you to fuss with it. Because suit jackets tend to bunch up when we are seated, grab the bottom of your jacket as you sit down and as much as possible, sit on it. This will keep the cloth around your shoulders lined up and smooth.

LINDA TRIPPS UP

Linda Tripp, the woman who tape-recorded her conversations with Monica Lewinsky, wanted to tell the world her side of the story. She wore a scarf around her neck to the interview.

It was an attractive scarf, but it kept slipping down—off her shoulders, down her back, or down her front. Whenever this happened, Tripp would dutifully reach up and reposition her scarf.

During this painful interview, she must have repositioned her scarf a few dozen times. Her fidgeting gave the impression of intense nervousness.

No doubt she was nervous—and for a whole host of reasons. Unfortunately, her nervous gestures sent a negative message. Viewers did not know whether they could believe her.

Linda Tripp must have known she would be nervous during the interview. If she had thought her situation through before hand, she might have chosen to dress in more comfortable, less demanding clothing—with no accessories like that scarf. Check your own clothing before beginning a videoconference. If you think you'll feel tempted to touch or adjust a piece of clothing, remove it or change.

42

Grooming

It is amazing how people can forget the most basic guidelines for looking fresh and alert. Here are some tips to keep yourself well groomed.

- Make sure your nails are clean and neatly trimmed. This is particularly true if you use a document camera. Every imperfection on your fingernails will be very visible.

- If you have a tendency to sport a five o'clock shadow, shave before your videoconference.

- Check the hair around your ears and neck; make sure it is neatly trimmed.

- Look at your clothing to make sure it is free from lint and dandruff.

- Keep a lint roller in your desk drawer so you can run it over your shoulders before you walk over to your conference.

- Bring an extra shirt or jacket with you if you run the risk of wrinkling yours before you begin your videoconference.

- Men, bring an extra tie with you, just in case something dribbles on the one you planned to wear for your conference.

- If your company has a videoconference studio in-house, consider buying a portable garment steamer for the room—so everyone can use it.

- Ask for feedback. Have someone check you to see that everything is in place.

OTHERS CAN DO ONLY
SO MUCH FOR YOU

A very entertaining example of grooming problems was shown on commercial television as an advertisement in 2001. The ad started with a senior-level executive walking to a meeting. His aides, using walkie-talkies, are sending messages to each other about his grooming mishaps.

"Snow on mountain. Snow on mountain," is the first message. Two aides miraculously appear, slap the executive on the shoulder and, without his noticing, rub off the dandruff that is sprinkling his shoulders.

After several similar grooming efforts, the man arrives now looking very executive-like, unknowingly taken care of by his aides. He reaches out to greet his guests, three impeccably groomed Japanese men. He smiles his big American smile, and a huge piece of green spinach completely covers his front teeth.

Others can only do so much for you. You have to look in the mirror yourself.

43

Your Gestures

Many videoconferencing systems today still use inadequate band-width to avoid the "herky-jerky" movement or ghosting (the resid-ual pattern that is left on a monitor) that accompanies narrow-bandwidth video transmission. This is particularly true with desk-top systems. Fortunately, high quality VC systems avoid most of these limitations.

Unless your bandwidth is broad enough to sustain hand gestures without making them appear jerky, minimize your gestures. In one videoconference, for example, a senior-level manager attempted to indicate a size he wanted by demonstrating with his hands. This ges-ture will work well when face-to-face, but with VC the results can be laughable. The receiving site was operating with a very slow frame rate so the distance being demonstrated came across as somewhere between one and two feet, not the precise distance the manager in-tended.

If you cannot control your moving hands, one thing you can do is to literally sit on them. Our favorite technique, though perhaps a bit extreme for most business settings, is one that Peta Peter used when she was a coanchor for an Australian television show. Peta normally speaks with her hands. Her habit is so deeply ingrained that to break this practice for television work, she sat on a large rubber band at-tached to both of her wrists. Every time she attempted to gesture with one hand, the rubber band would pull on her opposite hand, pre-venting the movement. She became very conscious of her gestures and quickly broke her habit while on camera.

Some nonverbal signals are effective and you should get into the habit of using them. Nod your head or smile in place of saying, "Yes," or "I see." By doing so, your gestures will avoid the problem of over-loading your VC system with vocal interruptions.

AVOIDING THE HERKY-JERKY

A story is told that in one of the world's premier financial organizations, the CEO understands how to work with videoconferencing technology. He is known to be a strong speaker who walks through the audience when he speaks and accompanies every word with vigorous gestures.

When he participates in a videoconference, however, he uses a completely different style. He speaks clearly, sits still, and rarely gestures.

This CEO knows that many of the organization's staff at distant locations around the world are connected to the Internet through low bandwidth and are watching the videoconference on their computers. The picture they see is very different from the quality that can be projected through multiple ISDN lines. Those watching through a low bandwidth connection are only able to see a fresh image every few seconds. Therefore, big movements are projected as spasmodic twitches.

The staff members of this organization have noticed the way their CEO shifts his style to accommodate the medium. His example is starting to have an impact on everyone's videoconference behavior. CEOs, take note: You are an "appearance" role model in the new videoconferenced world.

PART 6

Final Considerations

A Videoconference Checklist

The following checklist for conducting a videoconference can help you to be better prepared, to present more effectively, and to wrap up your meetings so they have long-term impact.

Before the Meeting

PARTICIPANTS

- Invite participants and confirm their availability. Make sure you know each other's videoconference and telephone numbers and e-mail addresses in case your virtual meeting is aborted.

- If your videoconference is formal, distribute a written agenda.

- Ask participants not to take any calls during the videoconference.

- Ask participants to create name cards so when they are on camera, everyone at off-site locations will be able to easily identify each other.

- Remind your participants that you want to start on time, so arriving early would be a good idea.

EQUIPMENT

- Check your video equipment to make sure it is working properly.

- Read the section in this book about working effectively with your equipment. For example, if you are bringing equipment into a room with windows, have the participants—not the camera—positioned facing the windows.

- Place the microphones so everyone projects clearly. Check for audio levels.

- Assign one person to be in charge of the camera. Choose an experienced operator who will do more than simply position the camera and leave it in a wide-angle position.

ELECTRONIC DOCUMENTS

- Prepare graphics to support your presentation, but keep them simple. Send them to participants in advance if appropriate. Make sure the text font is large and easy to read.

PRESENTATION

- Check to see that you are dressed appropriately. Make sure you are neat and clean.

- Determine if your meeting will be taped, and even then, assume it could be.

During the Meeting

ESTABLISHING GROUND RULES

- Start on time and finish on time.

- Indicate who will call whom to reconnect if your videoconference is aborted.

- Define the question-and-answer process. Explain the methods to be used to submit questions.

EQUIPMENT

- Point out the mute-button feature and tell participants when you want them to use it. Ask participants to mute their microphone if side conversations are necessary.

- Speak as you normally do. Avoid extraneous noises, such as clicking ballpoint pens and shuffling papers. Your microphone will amplify even the smallest sounds.

- Every once in a while, determine that everyone is tracking the meeting's content and that all can hear and see each other. People won't necessarily tell you.

PRESENTATION

- Look at people at your location—and the camera. Resist looking at the monitor. Avoid negative facial expressions; maintain a pleasant expression.

- Pay attention to how you sit, speak, and behave during your videoconference because others will be scrutinizing you carefully.

- If you use a document camera, be sure to use the main camera when you have finished data collaborating.

- Avoid any distracting hand gestures, nervous habits, and side conversations. Relax! Avoid strong negative emotions.

- Serve food during breaks, not while videoconferencing.

STARTING THE MEETING

- Review the meeting agenda.

- Welcome participants and ask everyone to introduce themselves. With name cards, they won't have to reintroduce themselves.

SPEAKERS

- Use different speakers and graphics during the meeting to avoid monotony.

- Be sure to create time for questions after someone has finished talking.

- If you are conducting the meeting at a slow speed (112 or 128 bits per second), explain the transmission delay. To maintain an orderly process in a multisite meeting, ask that participants identify themselves before raising a question.

After the Meeting

- Ask participants to evaluate the conference. You will probably learn something that will help you do better the next time.

- Follow up as required.

- Thank people for their participation.

- Send summaries so everyone has a written and public record of who agreed to do what.

45

A Legal Caveat

One final note: We have not discussed legal questions, but they are certain to loom large in the coming years as the world embraces videoconferencing as one of its common methods of communicating. We have identified two major issues that are not yet settled—at least no one that we have talked with seems to have clear-cut answers to these challenges. In fact, very few people have even begun to think about them. We do not intend our comments to represent legal advice and suggest that videoconference users check with their legal departments for relevant advice.

Copyright Issues

Copying other people's creations for our personal use is normally not a problem with copyright laws. You can, for instance, tape a song you hear on the radio for you own personal use. But you violate copyright laws when you put that music on your Web site. In business, if you place a graphic image that you downloaded from the Web into a presentation you are making to illustrate a point to a colleague, no one will protest. However, does the same standard apply if you data collaborate your document with a colleague, and it now is archived and stored on your company's intranet—for your other fifty thousand colleagues to see?

Recording Issues

The legal system has more or less sorted out the legalities around tape recording audio conversations. We are supposed to be clearly warned if a recording is being made when we are on the telephone. While laws vary from state to state, most people know that recording telephone conversations is illegal without first gaining the other person's permission.

Attorneys that we consulted all said that in the absence of specific laws that refer to videoconferencing, laws regarding tape recording apply equally well to videoconferences. Any videoconference can easily be stored—in effect tape-recorded—and yet people rarely issue warnings when this is being done. Who owns the recorded videoconference? Television studios clearly own their taped segments. They are copyright protected and the copyright is strongly enforced. In the case of VC, is the owner of a videoconference the person who initiated the call? And if I store a videoconference with you on my Web site, or even on my computer, do I need your written permission for this?

These are important questions and deserve serious consideration as we move into the world of videoconferencing. If you have any doubts, check with your organization's counsel to avoid legal exposure.

46

The Future of Videoconferencing

Unquestionably, we live in a world in which video has come to play a major role. Most people are comfortable with videos that monitor behavior for security purposes. Video cameras record all types of crimes: convenience store robberies, police abuse of citizens, accidents, bribes, plane hijackings, and even abuse of a child by a babysitter. The public looks forward to broadcasts of "accidental" videotape that shows an event captured live that the participants thought was private.

Now video has moved into the business world as a communication device. Future VC applications will be far-reaching and can only be imagined today. One day in the future it will be commonplace for us to eat a meal with a group of friends at one hotel dining room while another group of friends thousands of miles away dines at a second hotel—and it will appear as if we were all seated at one long table. (A group of California entrepreneurs is currently seeking venture capital for this application.)

Wireless technology will introduce even greater possibilities for videoconferencing. Think of all the wireless applications being used today; then imagine a future that includes video images. For example, videoconferencing on a PDA will happen. It is just a matter of time.

One difference between most video monitoring for security purposes and VC for business use is that with security monitors, we are passive in our relationship with the camera. Videoconferencing in the business world requires us to be active participants.

The question is whether we have the habits necessary for effective, active participation. Some people will never feel comfortable with the medium. Some will naturally do well with video communication; they will look good on camera without doing anything special. Others are going to have to work harder and learn new habits for visually projecting themselves through space. The good news is that people can improve their skills dramatically through reading, observation, and practice.

Young people growing up in today's world will no doubt have the easiest time adjusting to virtual events. Children will become accustomed to videoconferences perhaps by first seeing their grandparents from a distance. They will go through their school years with Mom and Dad checking up on them and their schoolwork while traveling on business. Children of divorced parents living in separate cities will have frequent and more regular visual contact with their distant parent. Judges are already approving parental moves out-of-state, and "virtual visitations" are considered adequate visits. The state of Michigan is planning the first "cybercourt," in which a judge and his or her clerk sits in a court room, virtually linking with lawyers and their clients. In courtrooms where a more limited use of VC is being made, the attorneys say that after a while they forget they are communicating through video.

Most of these new applications will be driven by the promise of saving time. One law professor contends that wired courtrooms can save anywhere from 25 percent to 50 percent of the time in a trial, just by eliminating the need to carry evidence from one group to another. Conducting arraignments by videoconference will save the cost and time of transporting prisoners from jails to courts. And taking witnesses' testimony by video will be convenient and timesaving. If nothing else, we will see more people willing to testify from remote distances.

Some of the applications will be driven by sharing talent across space. While still in the experimental stages, we can expect to see "videosurgery" become commonplace. In September 2001, two New York doctors operated on a patient in Strasbourg, France—3,900 miles away. Images of the woman's body were transmitted by two digital cameras. The surgeons grasped handles resembling surgical instruments. Their movements were translated and sent via a data stream (on high-speed fiber-optic cable under the Atlantic Ocean), with an astounding time delay of only eighty milliseconds. Lawrence Osborne of the *New York Times* describes this phenomenon as taking place in a "global operating room."[19]

The younger generation will undoubtedly become so comfortable with the medium that they will not be amazed by such examples, nor will they feel strange about shifting into VC mode. They will have a set of habits (many of which we can only imagine at this point) honed through feedback given to them over the years by parents, teachers, and friends. The challenge will be for those of us who are being introduced to VC in our adult lives.

Acquiring expertise with videoconferencing requires us to monitor our videoconference behaviors with care, never "winging it" with this potentially career-enhancing or career-breaking medium, showing respect for the power of VC equipment, and always being alert to the fact that whatever happens in a virtual meeting is amplified and may be recorded to haunt us forever.

No doubt we have a lot to learn. Do not give up if you experience a few failures. Learn from them. That is how good habits are formed. Remember, you will eventually come back to videoconferencing. The world will demand it of you.

Storyboarding

Storyboarding is a term co-opted from the field of film and video. It has now become a regular part of the planning of many videoconference programs, presentations, and even meetings—especially if the meeting has a significant visual component. Obviously, producing a storyboard would be overkill for informal meetings or for one-on-one webcasting.

Prior to a videoconference, a storyboard can be created and placed on the studio or meeting wall so everyone can see exactly who speaks when, about what, and which graphics are to be used. If you prefer to create a storyboard on your computer, you can use virtually any word-processing application to create one. You can clip and paste visual images to keep your storyboard lively. And you can print out copies for all participants. Software for storyboarding is also available. It can also be done with three-by-five-inch cards that are easy to move about with pins.

On the following page is a simple sample of a two-hour meeting of project managers with several component pieces and with three point-to-point locations.

TABLE A.1 A SAMPLE STORYBOARD

Time	Topic	Method	Graphics	System Cues	Participation
10:00–10:30	Update	Sites review results	MaxProj.doc Sum.doc Max.exl	Document camera Document camera Document camera	Tom Johnson, St. Louis Susan Longly, Atlanta George Harris, Houston
10:30–11:00	Discussion and prioritizing top three issues	Major challenges	White board	Voice-activated camera	All three locations Tom to capture notes
11:00–11:10	Break				All three locations
11:10–11:30	Brainstorm top three challenges	Solutions and implementation of action plans	Local computers Word software		All three locations operating independently with their teams
11:30–12:00	Report outs	Solutions and assigned responsibilities	Word software	Voice-activated camera Document camera	All three locations

105 Commonly
Mispronounced Words

While you are improving your image for videoconferencing, you might also make sure you are pronouncing words correctly. Listed below are 105 commonly used words that are frequently mispronounced. If you are insecure about your background, education, or accent, correctly pronouncing these words will help you appear as if you have an Ivy League education.

Some people argue that there is no one set way to pronounce a word. Others say that the way your boss pronounces the word is the correct way. Still others say that if others can understand you, it does not matter how you pronounce words. All this may be true, and if you hold these points of view, then you can skip this section. But for those of you who would like to make sure you are following standard pronunciation, the list follows.

The correct pronunciation of these words comes from the *Random House Dictionary of the English Language,* 2nd edition, Unabridged. We have used a simple phonetic system to indicate how the words should or should not be pronounced. First, the word is divided into syllables, and then its preferred pronunciation is given, followed by a short explanation of common mispronunciations. If this system is not clear to you, definitely check your dictionary.

By the way, these are words that Americans commonly mispronounce. Every nation has its own set of mangled words that go way beyond accents, which most people accept. For example, Australians rarely mispronounce "across," but they do have difficulties with the word "million." Instead of pronouncing it MILL-yen, even John Howard, the prime minister, says MILL-yu-un. It drives some Aussies crazy!

ABERRANT (a-ber-rant) *a-BEAR-ent.* Most people say AB-er-ent, so you will not sound out of place if you do too. But it is not the preferred pronunciation.

ABNORMAL (ab-nor-mal) *ab-NOR-mul.* Many people place the emphasis on the first syllable, AB-nor-mul.

ACADEMIA (ac-a-de-mi-a) *ak-a-DEEM-e-a.* A lot of people make the third syllable sound like *dem* in Democrat: ak-a-DEM-e-a.

ACCESSORY (ac-ces-sor-y) *ak-SES-or-ree.* Many people say A-SES-a-ree, changing the first syllable from *ak* to *a.*

ACCLIMATE (ac-cli-mate) *AK-le-mate.* Many place the emphasis on the second syllable and pronounce it a-CLI-mate. It sounds fancy, but it is not correct.

ACROSS (a-cross) *a-CROSS.* The mistake people make with this word is to pronounce it a-CROST.

ADMIRABLE (ad-mir-a-ble) *AD-mer-a-bel.* Some people make this word into two words: ad-MIRE-a-bel or admire-able.

AFFLUENCE (af-flu-ence) *AF-loo-ens.* It is common to place the emphasis on the second syllable: af-LOO-ens.

ALLEGED (al-leged) *a-LEG'D.* Many turn this two-syllable word into three syllables: a-LEG-ed.

ARCHETYPE (ar-che-type) *AR-ka-type.* Many turn this three-syllable word into two, dropping the middle *e.* Incorrectly pronounced, it sounds like ARK-type. Still others do not harden the *ch,* saying it ARCH-type.

ARCTIC (arc-tic) *ARK-tik.* This is a geographic name that is commonly mispronounced. Many people make it sound like: AR-tik. They drop the middle *c.*

ASSEMBLY (as-sem-bly) *a-SEM-bli.* Many people put an *s* sound with the first syllable: ass-SEM-bli.

ASSUAGE (as-suage) *a-SWAJ.* Many soften the *g* sound at the end of this word so it sounds like a-SWAZE.

ATHLETE (ath-lete) *ATH-leet.* People commonly add another syllable to this two-syllable word: ATH-a-leet.

BYZANTINE (byz-an-tine) *BIZ-un-teen.* The mistake made here is to place emphasis on the second syllable rather than the first. The word ends up sounding like biz-AN-tee-an.

CAPRICIOUS (ca-pri-cious) *ka-PRISH-as.* Many people put the *s* sound into the last syllable, hence ka-PRI-shus. It is a subtle mistake but annoying to people who know how to pronounce this word correctly.

CARIBBEAN (car-ibbe-an) *kar-a-BEE-un.* It is very common for people to make the "rib" a syllable, and they place the emphasis there: ka-RIB-bee-un.

CEMENT (ce-ment) *see-MENT.* A lot of people place the accent on the first syllable: SEE-ment.

CLIQUE (clique) *CLEEK.* Many pronounce the word as *click.* You will get by with that pronunciation, but it is not correct—according to the dictionary.

COMFORTABLE (com-fort-a-ble) *COM-fort-a-ble.* The two ways this word gets mangled are COMF-ter-ble or com-FERT-a-ble.

COMPARABLE (com-par-a-ble) *COM-per-a-bel.* This is the preferred pronunciation, though you can get by with placing the emphasis on the second syllable: com-PAIR-a-bel.

CONSORTIUM (con-sor-ti-um) *kun-SOR-she-um.* Many people leave the "tium" just as it reads, instead of turning it into an *sh* sound: kun-SOR-tee-um. And remember, there are four syllables, not three. Some people pronounce the word kun-SOR-shum.

CONTEMPLATIVE (con-tem-pla-tiv) *kun-TEM-ple-tiv.* The accent is on the second syllable instead of the third: kun-tem-PLAY-tiv.

CONTROVERSIAL (con-tro-ver-sial) *kon-tra-VUR-shal.* Many people incorrectly take the last syllable, *sial,* and turn it into two syllables: kon-tra-VUR-shee-al.

DAIS (da-is) *DAY-us.* It is not a DEE-as. The DAY-us, incidentally, is the raised platform (also called a podium) on which the lectern or head tables are placed. You stand on the DAY-us and speak from a LEC-turn.

DATA (da-ta) *DAY-ta.* This word causes lots of disagreement, but every dictionary we checked says DAY-ta is preferred. The word is divided in the middle of the four letters; it's not DAT-a.

DECIBEL (dec-i-bel) *DES-a-bell.* The mistake people make with this word is to turn that last syllable into a *bull* sound: DES-a-bull. Correctly pronounced, it's a *bell* sound.

DELUGE (del-uge) *DEL-ug'ja.* A *g* sound ends this word instead of DEL-uuze.

DISPARATE (dis-pa-rate) *DIS-par-ut.* The mistake that many make is to get the emphasis wrong: di-SPAR-ut.

DOESN'T (does-n't) *DUZ-unt.* You may be wondering who mispronounces this word. Actually, George W. Bush and many other Southerners say "duddn't" or DUD-ent.

EIGHTY (eight-y) *ATE-tee.* This word looks simple enough, but most people slur the last syllable: ATE-dee.

ELECTORAL (e-lec-tor-al) *a-LEK-tur-al.* Many people change the rear end of the word making it sound like a-lek-TOR-ee-al.

ENVELOPE (en-ve-lope) *en-vu-LOPE.* You can get away with saying AN-vu-lope, as they frequently do at the Oscars, but it is not the preferred pronunciation.

ENVOY (en-voy) *EN-voy.* The plain pronunciation is preferred, not AN-voy.

ERR (err) *UHR.* This one is so commonly mispronounced you will not sound out of place if you don't use the preferred pronunciation, which is *not* AIR.

ESPRESSO (es-pres-so) *ess-PRESS-oh.* You are not drinking ex-PRESS-oh—if you want to say it right.

FEBRUARY (Feb-ru-ar-y) *FEB-roo-air-y*. This is another commonly mispronounced common word. It is definitely not FEB-yoo-air-y.

FETE (fete) *FATE*. The word is pronounced the same as *fate,* not like your FEET.

FIGURE (fig-ure) *FIG-yer*. It is not FIG-ger, unless you happen to be British. When they talk about FIG-gers, they are really discussing FIG-yers.

FORMIDABLE (for-mi-da-ble) *FOR-mid-da-bel*. The emphasis should be placed on the first syllable—not the second. This is incorrect: for-MID-da-bel.

FORTE (for-te) *FOR-tay or FORT*. The pronunciation of this word varies, depending on what it means. When it means loud, as in music, it is FOR-tay. When discussing someone's strong point, use FORT. People frequently confuse the two words.

FOYER (foy-er) *FOY-ur*. An *ur* sound appears at the end of this word to be correct, instead of a hard *a* sound: FOY-a.

FUNGI (fun-gi) *FUN-jee*. This word gets mispronounced many ways including FUN-jai, or FUN-gee.

GALA (ga-la) *GAY-la*. Pronounce the word as in "we are having a gay old time," instead of GAL-lah.

GENUINE (gen-u-ine) *JEN-yu-un*. There is no *ine* sound at the end of this word: JEN-yu-ine.

GRIEVOUS (griev-ous) *GREE-vus*. There are only two syllables in this word. Therefore, the correct pronunciation is not GREE-vee-us.

HARASS (ha-rass) *huh-RASS*. The emphasis in this word is on the last syllable. You can probably get away with emphasizing the first syllable, but you would be wrong: HUH-rass.

HEGEMONY (he-gem-o-ny) *heh-GEM-ah-knee*. Many place the emphasis on the first three letters: HEDGE-ah-moan-ee. But look how the word is divided into syllables.

HEINOUS (hei-nous) *HAY-nuss.* The word only has two syllables, but people frequently turn it into three: HAY-knee-us.

HERB (herb) *URB.* In the United States, the *h* is silent; in the United Kingdom, Canada, and Australia, the *h* is pronounced, so the word sounds like the man's name Herb.

HOMICIDE (hom-i-cide) *Home-ah-SIDE.* The first syllable is pronounced like the word *home* and not HOM-ah-side.

HOSPITABLE (hos-pit-a-ble) *HOS-pi-tah-bull.* So many words are misprounced by virtue of where emphasis is placed. Such is the case here as well. The accent goes on the first syllable and not the second: hos-PIT-tah-bull.

IDEA (i-de-a) *eye-DEE-ah.* The mistake that many people make is to shorten the *a* sound at the end of the word. Sometimes you can barely hear them pronounce that sound at all: eye-DEE. The word has three clear syllables.

ILLUSTRATIVE (il-lus-tra-tive) *ih-LUS-tra-tiv.* You can get away with accenting the "tra," (ih-lus-TRAY-tiv) but the preferred pronunciation is to place the emphasis on the "lus."

INSOUCIANT (in-sou-ci-ant) *en-SOO-see-ant.* The trick here is to make the word four syllables, not three: in-SOO-shant. If you are good at videoconferencing, you should feel in-SOO-see-ant while participating in one!

INSURANCE (in-sur-ance) *in-SURE-uns.* The accent is definitely on the middle syllable and not on the first: IN-sure-uns.

IRREPARABLE (ir-rep-a-ra-ble) *ear-REP-ur-ah-bull.* Look at how the word is divided into syllables to avoid the common mispronunciation of putting a hard *pair* in the middle of the word: ear-rah-PAIR-ah-bull.

IRREVOCABLE (ir-rev-o-ca-ble) *ear-REV-ah-ke-bull.* Just like ear-REP-ur-ah-bull, the accent goes on the second syllable instead of ear-ra-VOKE-ah-bull or EAR-ra-voke-ah-bull.

JEWELRY (jew-el-ry) *JEW-el-ree.* This word gets mangled by many. They can pronounce "jewel," but they transpose the middle letters in this word so it sounds something like JEW-la-ree.

KILOMETER (kil-o-met-er) *kih-LAH-mih-ter.* Once again, we have a problem with emphasis. It is not KIL-o-meet-er or kil-o-MEET-er.

LAMBASTE (lam-baste) *lam-BASTE.* Correct pronunciation has the second syllable sound like basting a chicken instead of lam-BAST.

LARYNX (lar-ynx) *LAIR-inks.* This vocal organ you would be hard pressed to do without is not LAIR-nix.

LENGTH (length) *LENK'TH.* As in the word "strength," some people leave out the *g* sound. They say, LEN'TH.

LIAISON (li-ai-son) *Lee-aze-ZONE.* The main emphasis is placed on the final syllable, not the first: LEE-aze-zone. Think of the word *liase* (lee-AZE). Then it becomes clear where the emphasis should be.

LIBRARY (li-brar-y) *Lie-BREAR-ee.* A lot of people still omit that first *r,* making the word sound like LIE-bare-ee.

LONG-LIVED (long-lived) *LONG-LIVD.* The trick with this word is to give both parts of it equal emphasis. Most people put a heavier emphasis on the second half of the word: long-LIVD. Some even pronounce the "lived" as if it were the past tense of "live," or long-LIV-ED.

MENSTRUATION (men-stru-a-tion) *men-stroo-A-shun.* Maybe we mispronounce this one because we are uncomfortable with the word. It is not men-STRAY-shun.

MINUSCULE (mi-nus-cule) *MIN-ah-skyool.* This problem is subtle, but the word is not pronounced either as MIN-ih-skyool or mi-NIH-skew-al.

MISCHIEVOUS (mis-chie-vous) *MIS-cha-vus.* This word is so commonly mispronounced some will even fight you over how it should be pronounced. Look carefully at how it is spelled. Place your emphasis on the first syllable, instead of mis-CHEEV-ee-us.

MORES (mo-res) *MORE-aze.* There is definitely a long *a* at the end of the word. Do not soften it to MORE-us.

NAIVETE (na-ive-te) *nai-eve-TAY.* The emphasis is on the last syllable. Some people pronounce this word: nai-EVE-vah-tay. They actually put an extra syllable in the word.

NINETY (nine-ty) *NINE-tee.* Most people slur this word and do not create a definite *tee* sound at the end of the word. It comes out sounding like NINE-dee.

NUCLEAR (nu-cle-ar) *NOO-klee-ur.* This poor word is hopelessly mangled by many and frequently ends up sounding like NU-kew-lur.

NUPTIAL (nup-tial) *NUP-shul.* People make this one more difficult than it is. They turn it into a three-syllable word: NUP-shoo-ul.

OFFICIAL (of-fi-cial) *oh-FISH-ul.* The mistake that most people make is to emphasize the first syllable: OH-fish-ul. Correctly pronounced, the word has its emphasis on the second syllable. And that is oh-FISH-ul!

OFTEN (of-ten) *AHF-fen.* The *t* is silent in this word though many insist on verbalizing it as OFT-tun.

OPHTHALMOLOGY (oph-thal-mol-o-gy) *ahf-tha-MAH-low-gee.* As your eyes can see, it is not ahf-MAH-low-gee. An extra syllable is needed to be correct.

PENALIZE (pe-nal-ize) *PEEN-ah-lize.* The mistake people make is to pronounce the first syllable as in PEN-ah-lize. Prisoners go into a PEEN-ul (penal) institution so we can PEEN-ah-lize them.

PERCOLATE (per-co-late) *PERK-o-late.* There is no *u* in this word, though people commonly say PER-cu-late.

PIANIST (pi-an-ast) *pee-AN-ist.* Again, we have an accent problem. The emphasis is on the second syllable, instead of the first: PEE-ah-nist.

PLENITUDE (plen-i-tude) *PLEN-i-tude.* Some people put two extra *t* sounds into their pronunciation: PLENT-ti-tude.

POINSETTIA (poin-set-ti-a) *poin-SET-ee-ah.* Many people entirely omit the third syllable, pronouncing the word as poin-SET-ah.

PREFERABLE (pre-fer-a-ble) *PREF-er-ah-bull.* The common mistake with this word is another accent problem. The emphasis is on the first syllable instead of the second: pre-FUR-ah-bull.

PRESTIGIOUS (pres-tig-ious) *pree-STIJ-us.* The middle syllable is a short *i* and not a long one: pree-STEE-jus.

PREVENTIVE (pre-ven-tive) *pree-VEN-tive.* The mistake that people make here is to add an extra syllable, making the word "preventative": pree-VEN-ta-tive. It's pree-VEN-tive.

PRIVILEGE (priv-i-lege) *PRIV-ah-lidge.* Many people turn this into a two-syllable word (PRIV-lidge)—but it has three!

PROBABLY (prob-a-bly) *PRAH-bab-lee.* This word commonly gets mispronounced in several ways. You will hear it as PRAH-bull-ly, or PRAHB-lee, or even PROL-lee.

PROGRAM (pro-gram) *PRO-gram.* We hear people make two mistakes with this word. Some place the emphasis on the second syllable, pro-GRAM, and others change the second syllable from "gram" to "grum."

PRONUNCIATION (pro-nun-ci-a-tion) *pro-NUN-see-A-shun.* Some people put a "noun" in the middle of the word: pro-NOUN-see-A-shun.

REALTOR (re-al-tor) *REE-ul-ter.* This word is frequently pronounced as REE-la-ter. Real REE-ul-ters grimace when they hear that.

REMUNERATION (re-mu-ner-a-tion) *ree-mu-nuh-RAY-shun.* A lot of people change that first *m* into an *n* and the word comes out sounding like this: ree-new-mer-RAY-shun.

SILICON (sil-i-con) *SIL-ah-kun.* The last syllable is not "cone" as in SIL-ah-cone. Poor SIL-ah-kun Valley is frequently mispronounced!

SPECIES (spe-cies) *SPEE-shez.* Put a definite sh sound in that second syllable—or you are mispronouncing the word. It is not SPEE-sees.

SPONTANEITY (spon-ta-ne-i-ty) *Spon-ta-KNEE-ah-tee.* The third syllable has a *knee* sound to it, rather than a *nay* sound, spon-ta-NAY-ah-tee. You can undoubtedly pronounce this one either way, but the preferred way is to put a *knee* in spon-ta-KNEE-ah-tee.

STATUS (sta-tus) *STAY-tus.* Many people make the mistake of making the first syllable *stat* as in STAT-us.

SUBLIMABLE (sub-li-ma-ble) *SUB-lih-mah-bull.* The trick here is to place your emphasis on the first syllable. Then it should come out all right. Many people place their emphasis on the second syllable: Sub-LIM-ah-bull.

SUCCINCT (suc-cinct) *sah-SINGKT.* This is another example of misplaced emphasis. The accent goes on the second syllable, not the first: SAH-singkt. And the *cs* are soft, so it's not SUCK-singkt.

SUPPOSED (sup-posed) *sah-POZD.* The mistake made here is to turn this two-syllable word into three syllables. It is commonly pronounced so it sounds like sah-POZ-ed.

SUPPOSEDLY (sup-posed-ly) *sah-POZD-ed-lee.* You would think that the people who mispronounce "supposed" would carry their mistake over to this word. Then they would have it right. Instead, they say sah-POSE-ah-blee.

TOWARD (to-ward) *TORD.* This two-syllable word is preferably pronounced as if it had one syllable instead of as too-WARD. This is what makes English pronunciation so difficult—there are millions of exceptions.

TRANSIENT (tran-sient) *TRAN-shent.* Many attempt to make this two-syllable word into three, TRAN-see-unt. Preferred pronunciation is just two.

VASE (vase) *VAYS.* Preferred American pronunciation is with the long *a*. In Great Britain, you might try VAHZE to speak like the natives. Both are correct within their own cultures.

VEGETABLE (veg-e-ta-ble) *VEG-tah-bull*. This four-syllable word is pronounced correctly as if it only as three syllables, instead of VEH-jha-tah-bull.

VETERINARIAN (vet-er-i-nar-i-an) *veh-tur-ih-NAIR-ree-an*. Some people leave out one of the syllables so it sounds like vetri-NAIR-ree-an.

NOTES

1. As quoted in "Down to Business, Virtually," *The Washington Times,* 11 October 2001.

2. M. Anthony Carr, "U.S. Is Getting Wired for Telecommuting," *The Washington Times,* 11 January 2002.

3. Terry Brock, interview by the authors, Las Vegas, January 6, 2002.

4. "New Research Report from Wainhouse Research Says Market for Audio, Video, and Web Conferencing Services to Reach $9.8 billion by 2006, up from $2.8 billion in 2000," Wainhouse Research Press Release, 8 January 2002.

5. March 2002, e-mail exchange with Roopam Jain, Strategic Analyst-Conferencing, with Frost and Sullivan. Jain's research covers data available through February 2002.

6. Source: http://www.saitama.med.or.jp/tvnet/sld003.html. This information was translated for us by Yoshi Asilano.

7. Source: "Turbulent Times Increase Virtual Meetings," *Business Wire,* 13 December 2000.

8. "Down to Business, Virtually," *The Washington Times,* 11 October 2001.

9. Howard Feiertag, "Technology Delivers, but Sales People Are Here to Stay," *Hotel and Motel Management Association,* 211 (1996) 16–17.

10. Malcolm Gladwell, *The Tipping Point: How Little Things Can Make a Big Difference,* Little Brown & Company, 2000.

11. Jay Koenigsberg, interview by the authors, Las Vegas, Nevada, February 2, 2002.

12. As quoted in Joel Garreau, "Closeness at a Distance; Can Virtual Technology Ever Achieve That Human Touch?" *The Washington Post,* 28 November 2000, pp. C01.

13. Ibid.

14. Quoted in Sherwood Ross, "Workplace: Internet Seen Falling Short for Global Teamwork," *Reuters Business Reports,* 5 November 2001.

15. As quoted in Roxanna Guilford, "Hotels Tap into Videoconference Meeting Trend," *Atlanta Business Chronicle,* 26 October 1998.

16. As quoted in Kate Kilperin, "The Economic Fall-out: Sales Boom for Video Conferences," *Independent on Sunday,* 23 Sept 2001, p. 3.

17. Vin D'Agostino, telephone conversation with the authors, January 28, 2002.

18. Sharon Jackle, interview by the authors, Honolulu, Hawaii, February 7, 2002.

19. Lawrence Osborne, "The Year in Ideas: A to Z," *New York Times Magazine,* 104, 9 December 2001.)

Bibliography

Several books other than the ones listed below have been written about videoconferencing. Most of them are no longer in print. Rather than tease our readers with books that are practically impossible to find, we have focused on the books that you can easily purchase on the Web.

Diamond, Lynn and Stephanie Roberts. *Effective Videoconferencing: Techniques for Better Business Meetings.* Menlo Park, Calif.: Crisp Publications, 1996. While dated, this book contains good material about the technology involved in videoconferencing. The authors have married the techniques of videoconferencing and running effective meetings. They do not cover presentation style in any great depth.

Duran, Joe John and Charlie Sauer. *Mainstream Videoconferencing: A Developer's Guide to Distance Multimedia.* Boston: Addison-Wesley, 1997. This is primarily a technical book, an introduction to "group" videoconferencing and the emergence of desktop videoconferencing. Six hundred pages long, it is a "must have" for anyone who needs to cover the technical side of videoconferencing.

Hansell, Kathleen, Ed. *The Teleconferencing Manager's Guide.* White Plains, N.Y.: Knowledge Industry Publications, 1989. A guide to technologies, applications, and techniques. The book considers business needs, marketing and implementation problems, and costs. It contains a short bibliography.

Rhodes, John and Brad Caldwell. *Videoconferencing for the Real World.* Wobum, Mass.: Butterworth-Heinemann, 2001. A step-by-step guide for the selection, installation, and operation of an effective videoconferencing solution, from desktop systems, set-top systems, and rollabout systems to complete room systems.

Rosen, Evan. *Personal Videoconferencing.* Greenwich, Conn.: Manning Publications Co., 1996. This book is one of the most complete books on videoconferencing. Evan Rosen attempts to position videoconferencing for the twenty-first century. He even makes up a new word (which has not stuck) to cover the field: "collabicate," which he defines as collaborating and communicating.

Rosen covers the conceptual aspects of the field and focuses heavily on data collaboration; he discusses the challenges and the opportunities in the field. If your intent is to fully understand VC technology, put this book on your reading list. The one aspect he does not cover is how to look good while on camera.

Schaphorst, Richard. *Videoconferencing and Videotelephony: Technology and Standards.* Boston: Artech House, 1999. Schaphorst's book is a compendium of technical information about videoconferencing.

Wilcox, James R. *Videoconferencing: The Whole Picture,* 3d ed. Gilroy, Calif.: Telecom Books, 2000. This book is an introduction to the technology of videoconferencing, how to buy it, and how to evaluate your needs.

Useful Terms to Know

ANALOG. The way some video, voice, and data is transferred over communication systems. Analog transmission is used over traditional analog telephones lines and usually does not provide high enough bandwidth capabilities for clear videoconferencing. By now, most analog lines have been replaced with digital lines.

ASP (application service provider). An organization that hosts software applications on its own servers. Customers can connect to the server to use the software or other services and technology they provide.

ATM (asynchronous transfer mode). A technology for transporting voice, video, and data. ATM is most commonly used as an Internet backbone technology for ISPs, telecom carriers, and large private enterprises. It is less commonly used for LANs and WANs.

BACKBONE. Large, high-speed transmission lines used to connect the Internet and networks over large geographic areas.

B and D CHANNELS. ISDN, T-lines and DSL lines contain different channels such as B and D channels. B channels or, bearer channels, are used to carry voice, data, and video. D channels, or delta channels, direct and control the signals to B channels.

BANDWIDTH. The amount of information that can pass between sites. It is measured in bits per second such as Kbps (kilobytes per second) and Mbps (megabytes per second).

BONDING. Generally the connecting of channels within lines such as in ISDN, T-lines, and DSL lines. "Bonding protocol" is an industry standard protocol for connecting B channels in lines.

BRIDGE. In simple terms, a mechanism that connects devices of compatible protocols together, such as networks. A MCU (multipoint control unit) is a type of bridge.

BRIDGING SERVICE. A service used to connect sites in a multipoint videoconference.

BRI-ISDN (basic rate interface ISDN). This refers to an ISDN line in which 64 Kbps B channels from two ISDN lines are combined together to form a single, higher speed connection of 128 Kbps. (Each regular ISDN line contains one "B" channel of 64 Kbps.) When two BRI-ISDN lines are installed, speed increases to 256 Kbps. When three BRI-ISDN lines are installed, speed increases to 384 Kbps, and so on. Because these lines go through the public-switched telephone network, they are subject to regular telephone fees per minute of use and can be quite expensive since they use multiple telephone lines.

CABLE INTERNET. The process of using cable television to connect a computer to an ISP (Internet service provider) thus bypassing both telephone lines and the public-switched telephone network. The speed of cable Internet is heavily influenced by the number of customers using the local ISP at the same time.

CASCADING. Also referred to as "cascaded videoconference." In a multipoint videoconference connected over ISDN lines and extending over a large geographic area (for example, internationally between Europe and North America), the sites in one location will form one group and use a single MCU to create their own videoconference. In such a videoconference, MCUs will communicate with one another, thus reducing the amount of long distance or multiple overseas telephone calls. Overall quality of the videoconference is also improved.

CIRCUIT SWITCHED. A networking technology for transferring data used on analog-based telephone and ISDN lines. Not used on IP-centric connections, where packet switched technology is used.

CO (central office). Also known as a "switching center." This is the local telephone company's center where a lot of the DSL, T-lines, and ISDN lines are transferred.

CODEC (encoder-decoder). A device that compresses and turns audio and video data into digital data and prepares it for transmission. On the receiving end, the codec decompresses and decodes the digital data back into audio and video data. Codecs transmit and receive simultaneously. A higher quality codec will help increase the quality of videoconferencing and offer many additional capabilities.

COLLABORATIVE COMPUTING. The sharing, viewing, and editing of real-time data between computers, such as charts, diagrams, applications, and data. "Data conferencing" and "data collaboration" are general terms used to describe collaborative computing. Different types of data collaboration include screen sharing, screen annotation, white boarding and application sharing. The terms are fluid and actually may mean different things to different people. It will take a few more years for the terms in collaborative computing to become firmly defined.

COMPRESSION. Compressing or squeezing the amount of information, or bits, so data can be more easily transferred or stored.

COMPUTER-MEDIATED COMMUNICATION. An umbrella term for all types of communication via computers, such as electronic conferencing, videoconferencing, Web casting, and chat.

COPY-STAND CAMERA. A camera that is built on a graphics copy-stand designed for sharing and transmitting images, photographs, spreadsheets, and graphs in a videoconferencing system.

DATA CONFERENCING/DATA COLLABORATION. *See* collaborative computing.

DESKTOP VIDEOCONFERENCING. Common parlance for the use of a personal computer to serve as a videoconferencing unit. A small camera is connected to the computer monitor. This is the most affordable videoconferencing unit and very easy to use. The small camera size limits use to only one or two people in front of a camera at one time. Desktop videoconferencing can also be used for data conferencing.

DIGITAL. The way some video, voice, and data are transferred over communication systems (*See* Analog). Digital transmission is used on digital telephone lines such as ISDN, T-lines, and DSL.

DOCUMENT CAMERA. A camera that is focused exclusively on documents needing to be transmitted.

DSL (digital subscriber line). A technology that greatly increases the speed of a digital line. Referred to as a DSL line or DSL. DSL lines use packet-switched technology and are IP based. Different types of DSL include ADSL, VDSL, and HDSL. Each one differs greatly in downstream and upstream speeds, which range from 144 Kbps to as high as 52 Mbps. DSL speeds, unlike cable modems, do not fluctuate based on the number of people accessing the Web in the local geographic area, but by the distance between the customer's site and the telephone company's central office. DSL lines are similar to T-lines in that they are IP based. This means that once the data reaches the telephone company's central office, the data bypasses the public-switched telephone network and connects directly to the user's ISP.

DUPLEX. The transmission of data. With full-duplex, data is two-way and simultaneous. With half-duplex, transmission is limited to one direction at a time. Full-duplex audio enables remote sites to speak simultaneously without losing contact.

ECHO CANCELER. A device that minimizes room echoes.

E-LINES. E-1, E-2, E-3, and so on, lines are the European equivalent of the T-1, T-2, T-3, and so on, lines used in North America, Japan, Korea, and many other countries.

ETHERNET. The most widely used technology for transporting voice, video, and data over LANs. Its standard protocol is IEEE 802.3. Also known as the IEEE 802.3 network.

FIREWALL. Software for keeping a network secure. When H.323 networks are communicating with one another, whether through videoconferencing, audio, or e-mail, a site has access to the IP address of the site it is communicating with. One site may possibly gain access to private information beyond the IP address or accidentally or purposely leave unwanted information, such as a virus. Firewalls help keep this information and the communication secure by filtering out unwanted packets of information and limiting access to details of the network. A proxy is another fundamental method of keeping a network secure. Typically, firewalls and proxies are used together to increase security.

FPS (frames per second). The number of frames per second that are displayed in a video image. For a clear image, most videoconferencing needs to be thirty FPS.

GATEKEEPER. A device that performs a multitude of functions within a network including translating IP addresses into actual people's names; performing call authorization, routing, transferring, and forwarding; and handling billing information.

GATEWAY. A device that performs protocol conversion between IP networks and legacy (older) networks. For example, a gateway will receive and transcode an H.320 protocol stream from an ISDN line and then convert it into an H.323 protocol stream and send it to the IP network and vice versa.

GRAPHICS CAMERA. A camera with high resolution capabilities.

H.320 STANDARD. A communication protocol standard among video-conferencing, electronic, and computer systems and networks. This is an older standard preceding the H.323 and works on older video-conferencing systems, most of which are only capable of working on ISDN lines from the VC site they are connecting from. Some of these videoconferencing units can be upgraded to use H.323 standards. See H323 standard.

H.323 STANDARD. A standard intercommunication protocol among videoconferencing, electronic, and computer systems and networks used over IP. Supersedes the H.320 standard, which is used for ISDN.

INTERNET2. The high-speed network administered by UCAID (University Corporation for Advanced Internet) for government, research, and academic use. It represents the next generation of the Internet, which is designed for high speed exchange with much higher QoS.

IP (Internet Protocol). A communications protocol over the Internet referred to as TCP/IP. The transmission control protocol (TCP) provides the transport functions; the IP provides the routing functions. In videoconferencing terms, IP describes videoconferencing that uses the Internet as opposed to using traditional telephone lines as ISDN technology does. T-lines and DSL lines (they are IP based) have much greater bandwidth capability and potentially lower cost than traditional telephone-line ISDN-based videoconferencing. However, IP based lines do not always transfer video information as clearly as ISDN lines because of QoS (quality of service) limitations. ISDN lines are technologically very adept at sending and receiving video information but have limited bandwidth. But the future of videoconferencing is definitely in IP. There are no per minute phone charges and the quality and QoS problems are improving very quickly.

ISDN (integrated services digital network). ISDN is an international telecommunications standard providing connections between a customer's site and the outside telephone network. It uses circuit-switching technology, as opposed to the more advanced packet-switching technology. ISDN can deliver voice, data, and video. It is important to note that an ISDN connection is not IP (Internet Protocol) based, as T-lines and DSL are. Once the ISDN line data reaches the telephone company's central office, it goes through a public-switched telephone network and then eventually connects to the other network or VC system. ISDN is currently the most common way videoconferencing systems communicate with each other. ISDN lines are transmitted through the public-switched networks, making them susceptible to taking electronic "hits" or events that can interrupt a call. ISDN lines have low bandwidth. One common way of getting around the low bandwidth drawback is for a user to install a BRI-ISDN line, which bonds several ISDN lines together and thereby greatly increases bandwidth. The advantage ISDN lines have over T-lines, DSL, and cable lines is that the connection quality is sometimes more consistent during a videoconference and is more readily available than IP connections. The disadvantage of ISDN lines is that the cost can sometimes be quite expensive as multiple phone lines are being used.

ITU (International Telecommunications Union). A group in Geneva, Switzerland, that sets computer communication protocol standards such as the H.320 and H.323.

KBPS (kilobytes per second). Used for measuring transmission speed on communication systems. It is equivalent to one thousand bits per second.

LAN (local area network). Communication networks used within an office complex, department, or other small geographic area.

LAST MILE/LOCAL LOOP. The connection between the customer and the telephone company's central office.

LATENCY. In general terms, the time between initiating a request for data and the actual time of transfer. In videoconferencing terms, it most commonly refers to the transmission delays in a packet-switched network.

MBPS (megabytes per second). Used for measuring transmission speed on communication systems. It is the equivalent to one million bits per second.

MCU (multipoint control unit). A device that connects multiple videoconferencing sites together. It is a type of bridge. With H.323 systems, the MCU consists of a multipoint controller (MC) and a multipoint processor (MP). The MC checks the other sites' capabilities and sends the audio, video, and data streams. The MP processes the information.

NATIVE RESOLUTION. Picture quality that is the same for the VC system sending the picture as it is for the nonlocal site. This enables each group to see exactly what the other is seeing.

OMNIDIRECTIONAL MICROPHONES. A microphone that is capable of picking up sounds from all sides.

OVERHEAD. Usually refers to "packet overhead," where each packet of information sent and received over an IP network contains a "header" or destination address that requires approximately forty bytes. As a result, a videoconference running over IP at a bandwidth of 384 Kbps, will need to give up some of its bandwidth to accommodate the bytes taken up in the header. The total amount of bandwidth accommodated is usually not enough to visibly affect the overall quality of the videoconference. There is no overhead in ISDN videoconferencing.

PACKET SWITCHED. A networking technology that breaks up messages into smaller packets of data used over IP. Each packet contains a destination address and does not have to travel a similar path. Packet technology is not used in ISDN lines, where circuit-switching technology is used.

PIXILATION. When a VC call takes a "hit." The need for the screen to regenerate all of the pixels to return to a smooth picture.

POINT-TO-POINT. Videoconferencing in which one site connects to another site. Video and audio may be one- or two-way.

POP (point of presence). The point at which the long-distance carrier connects to the local telephone carrier.

POTS (plain old telephone service). Analog, narrow-band, circuit-switched local telephone service. For example, an analog dial-up modem uses POTS.

PREVIEW MONITOR. Displays the video or images going to other videoconferencing sites. Remember that what you see on your preview monitor will not be exactly the same as what the other sites see on their monitors.

PRI-ISDN (primary rate interface ISDN). A particular type of ISDN line that has twenty-three B channels, unlike a regular ISDN line, which only has one B channel. These channels can be connected together to increase the speed of videoconferencing up to 1.472 Mbps. Of course, the price is higher than regular ISDN as more phone lines are being used.

PRIVATE NETWORK. A network of computer servers or videoconferencing systems that are linked together over point-to-point lines. This eliminates the need to go to an outside network every time information is communicated and greatly increases the quality and speed of information that is transmitted.

PROXY. Also called "proxy server." A device for keeping a network secure. Information going from a network to the Internet and vice versa can go through a proxy server. The proxy server closes the straight path between the Internet and the network and also limits IP address information and details of the network, thus making the network more secure. Typically, firewalls and proxies are used together to increase security.

PSTN (public-switched telephone network). The worldwide voice telephone network.

QoS (Quality of Service). The mechanisms in a data communications system that determine the quality and types of information sent and received. For example, video, voice, and data information packets have different characteristics and the QoS helps in determining which one is which and how to receive and send the information. Voice and video transferred over IP lines require a higher level of QoS than data transferred over IP lines. Information transferred over ISDN does not have QoS issues. QoS problems coupled together with bandwidth fluctuations can cause the quality to go up and down during a videoconference. But the technology is now getting so strong that QoS is quickly becoming less and less of an issue.

ROLLABOUT. A unit that usually sits inside a wheeled cabinet to serve as a videoconferencing unit. It will contain one or two monitors and a pan-tilt-zoom camera (a camera that zooms and moves in both vertical and horizontal planes). It is typically more powerful than a set-top system but slightly more difficult to operate. These systems are good for groups of six or more people at one site.

ROOM SYSTEM. A high-end videoconferencing unit with a large screen and cameras. The room is typically echo and sound proofed. Good for large groups.

SET-TOP. A compact unit containing a camera, microphone, and speaker that sits on top of a television set or monitor. It is very easy to use, reasonably priced, but sometimes lacking in capabilities. It is only good for very small groups of people to be around the camera at one time.

SONET (synchronous optical networks). A fiber-optic transmission system and standard.

SPLIT-SCREEN CAPABILITY. A system that can show multiple sites simultaneously. This can be done on one computer or on two monitors side by side.

STORAGE AND TRANSMISSION CAPACITIES.

SPACE	BITS/BYTES	POWER OF 10
kilo	thousand	3
mega	million	6
giga	billion	9
tera	trillion	12
peta	quadrillion	15
exa	quintillion	18
zetta	sextillion	21
yotta	septillion	24

STREAMING VIDEO. Video transmission over a data network, widely used to transmit video broadcasts.

T-1, T-2, T-3 (T-lines). A technology that greatly increases the speed of a digital line. Referred to as T-lines, it uses packet-switched technology and is IP based. T-1 has speed capabilities of up to 1.54 Mpbs; T-2 up to 6.314 Mbps; and T-3 up to 44.736 Mpbs. But one should keep in mind that there are partial and full T-lines. For example, a partial T-1 line only has a speed of 128 Kbps, but it would still be referred to as a T-1 line. Since T-lines are IP based, once the data reaches the telephone company's central office, the data bypasses the public-switched telephone network and connects directly to the user's ISP. T-1 lines, in particular, are also widely used to connect computers and systems within a private network, LAN, or WAN.

T.120 STANDARD. A standard for the exchange of data and graphic images among personal computers and videoconferencing systems set by the ITU (International Telecommunications Union).

TOKEN RING. One of the latest technologies used for transporting voice, video, and data over LANs. Its standard protocol is IEEE 802.5. Is also known as the IEEE 802.5 network.

UNIDIRECTIONAL (cardiod) MICROPHONES. Microphones that pick up sounds from a narrow zone.

USB (universal serial bus). A hardware interface (usually on the back of computers or electronic devices) to connect peripherals such as keyboards, mice, scanners, and VC equipment.

VIDEOCONFERENCING. A type of virtual meeting in which you can both see and interact with another remote site in real time.

VIDEOPHONES. A special portable device with a small screen and camera for videoconferencing. This is a low-end system usually running with a bandwidth between 64 and 128 Kbps, which greatly limits its capabilities. They are rarely used anymore, if at all.

VOICE-ACTIVATED CAMERA. Cameras that are linked to microphones and automatically turn to the person who is speaking.

VPN (virtual private network). A private network that at some point in the connection will use public or insecure networks (such as the Internet or backbone lines), ensuring security by various encryption or authentication means.

WAN (wide area network). A communication network used over a wide geographic area within cities or between different countries.

WEBCASTING. Streaming video over the Internet. All communication—audio, video, and data—is unidirectional.

WEB CONFERENCING. A set of software applications (e.g. WebEx, PlaceWare, Paltalk) that use Web technology to host meetings or presentations. With such conferences, the camera feed is unidirectional, though voice and written communication can go in both directions. Also referred to as "net conferencing."

WHITE BOARD. A drawing space on a monitor that allows sites in a multipoint videoconference to make simultaneous changes to a document. Also called "white boarding."

Index

A

Addams, Jill, 1
after the meeting, 128
agendas
  meeting, 48–49
  personal, 50–51
  timing, 61
alternatives to videoconferencing,
  36–37
amplification, problems of, 87, 101,
  114
anger, 94–95
anxiety, 110–111
appearance
  clothing, 78, 79, 92–93
  and comfort, 21
  grooming, 118–119
  hairstyles, 114–115
  jewelry, 106–107
  personal, 49
  posture, 100
  wearing makeup, 102–103
  See also behavior; boredom
assuming you're live, 96–97, 100
attendees. *See* participants
awareness level during videoconferences, 71

B

background noise, 72–73
backgrounds
  color of, 92–93
  distracting, 71, 78

bald men, 102
Barlow, Janelle, 13, 69, 89
Barlow, John Perry, 29
Barlow, Lewis, 13, 101
behavior
  angry, 94–95
  anxious, 111
  distracting, 90–91, 114, 120–121
  with food and water, 88–89
  genuine, 110
  low-class, 88
  neutral expressions, 100–101
  telephone-like, 20–22
  toward audience, 49
  when sick, 104–105
believability, 113
Bell Labs, 9
beverages, 88
bloopers, 81
body language, 18
boredom, 28, 48–49, 101
breakdowns of equipment, 71
breakout sessions, 58
breaks, 65, 88
Brock, Terry, 9
Bush, George H. W., 101, 105
Bush, George W., 109

C

cameras, 74–75
Carlson, David, xi
Carter, Jimmy, 109
Charles, Prince of Wales, 111

checklists for managing videoconferences
  after the meeting, 128
  electronic documents, 126
  equipment, 125–127
  establishing ground rules, 126
  participants, 125
  the presentation, 126, 127
  speakers, 127–128
  starting the meeting, 127
Clinton, Bill, 77, 101, 109, 113
closing the meeting, 64–65
clothing, 78, 79, 92–93, 116–117
collaboration, 3–5
color
  of clothing, 92–93
  of documents, 82
commonly mispronounced words, 108, 137–164
communication
  intimacy of, in videoconferencing versus other forms, 29–30
  and miscommunication, 63
  subtleties of, 27–29
comparisons
  videoconferences/face-to-face meetings, 40–41
  videoconferences/in-person meetings, 23–24
  videoconferencing/no meeting, 35
complementary service, videoconferencing as, 31–32
conservation issues, 16
cost control, 12–14, 36–37
cultural issues, 62–63

D

D'Agostino, Vincent, 45
data collaboration, 3–5
decision making
  alternatives to videoconferencing, 36–37
  methods of, in your organization, 18
  objectives of using videoconferencing, 39

taping the conference, 80–81
videoconferencing or face-to-face meetings, 40–41
  videoconferencing or teleconferencing, 42–43
  videoconferencing versus using other tools, 36–37
decor, 90
delays in visual or auditory signal, 19
desk videoconferencing unit, 75
Diana, Princess, 111
disagreements, 100
discipline during meetings, 18
discussions at remote sites, 66
disruptions, 55
distractions
  backgrounds, 71, 78
  behavior, 90–91, 114
  clothing, 92–93, 117
  eating/drinking on camera, 88, 90
  gestures, 120–121
  moving your legs, 90
  off-camera, 91
documents
  checklist for managing, 126
  enhancing, for viewing, 82–83
drinking beverages on camera, 88
dual-monitor systems, 5

E

eating during conferences, 88, 89
electronic documents
  checklist for managing, 126
  enhancing, for viewing, 82–83
e-mail
  after conferences, 66
  questions/comments via, 56, 58
emotions, handling
  anger, 94–95
  anxiety, 110–111
  hostility, 56
environment, protection of, 16
equipment, 10–11, 71, 125–127
etiquette, microphone, 72–73
evaluations, for lessons learned, 68–69

expectations
  for e-mail versus videoconferences, 71
  setting reasonable, 47
expertise, acquiring, 133
eyes, using your, 112–113

F

face-to-face meetings, xii, xiii
  advantages of, 14–15
  versus videoconferencing, 40–41
  videoconferencing as supplement to, 31
failure
  contingency plans for equipment problems, 84–85
  of global teams, 30
falling asleep, 59
Fedderson, Darr, 13
feedback, asking for, 58
feet, moving your, 90
Field, Sally, 53
filler phrases, 74
finishing, on-time, 61
flowers, 90
following up after meetings, 66–67, 128
font sizes for slides, 82
food, 88, 89
formality of videoconferencing, 38–39
Funt, Allan, 81
future of videoconferencing, 131–133

G

Garner, Jennifer, 73
Gates, Bill, 29, 87
gestures
  managing your, 120–121
  rude, 63
  waving goodbye, 64
  waving hello, 52
Gladwell, Malcolm, 16
global teams, failure of, 30
Godi, Ann, 31
Gore, Al, 95, 109
Grace, Peter, 88

greeting attendees, 52
grooming, 118–119
ground rules, 53, 54, 126
group discussions, 100–101
guidelines for moderators, 54–55

H

habits
  changing, for virtual meetings, xi–xii
  learning the new, 131–132
  need for new, 17
hairstyles, 114–115
hostility, 56, 94–95
House, Chuck, 25, 35
Howard, John, 137
Humphrey, Hubert, 103

I

illness, handling, 104–105
impressions, making first, 53
information technology, 11
in-person meetings
  recording, 19
  subtleties of, 27–29
  versus videoconferences, 23–24
interactivity, 20–21
international videoconferences, 62–63
interruptions
  in visual or auditory signal, 19
  vocal, 120
intimacy of communication, 29–30
introductions, 52
ISDN (Integrated Services Digital Network), 13

J

Jackle, Sharon, 50
Jain, Roopam, 9
jewelry, 106–107
Johnson, Lyndon, 109

K

Kennedy, John F., 103
King, Larry, 56
Koenigsberg, Jay, 17

L

lapel microphones, 73
late attendees, 61
legal issues
    copyrights, 129
    cybercourt, 132
    ownership of videotape, 130
    recording the meeting, 129–130
    storage of videotapes, 130
legs, moving your, 90
"lessons learned" evaluations, 68–69
Lewin, David, 30
lighting, 78–79
limitations of videoconferences, 25–27, 31
looking into the camera, 74, 110
lunch breaks, 65

M

makeup, 102–103
managers, expectations for, 2
McLuhan, Marshall, 71
memos, 67
men
    jewelry for, 106–107
    makeup for, 102
microphones
    live, 96
    tips for using, 72–73
    voice-activated, 71
miscommunication, 63
mispronounced words, 108, 137–164
missteps, avoiding, 45
moderators
    bored, 59
    closings by, 64
    guidelines for, 54–55
    handling hostility, 57
Morris, Anna, 2
multisite meetings, 38
Murphy's Law, 84–85, 97

N

negative emotions, 94–95
negative remarks, 96
nerves, controlling, 110–111, 117

news media, 45
Nixon, Richard, 103, 109
nonverbal signals, 18, 120
note-taking during conferences, 66, 101

O

objectives, prioritizing, 50
offscreen attendees, 52
on-camera zone, 74
one-way transmissions, 52
opening the conference, 52–53
overuse issues
    of bells and whistles, 83
    of videoconferencing, 38

P

panel discussions, 100–101
paperless offices, 30
participants
    addressing, 62
    checklist for managing, 125
    greeting attendees, 52
    late arrivals, 61, 98
    no-shows, 99
    offscreen attendees, 52
    thanking, 64, 66, 128
participation, 58–59
pauses, appropriate, 74
pen twirling, 90
Perot, Ross, 53, 95, 109
personal goals/agendas, 50
Peter, Peta, 107, 120
Philbin, Regis, 115
plants, 90
Polycom, 11
posture, 100
power, giving up, 69
preparation for videoconferencing
    controlling your nerves, 110–111
    lack of, 50
    practicing with TelePrompTers, 76
    questions for, 46–47
    winging it, 45
presentations, checklist for managing, 126, 127

problems
  of amplification, 87
  avoiding missteps, 45
  breakdowns of equipment, 71
  failures of global teams, reasons
    for, 30
  late starts, 98
  of lighting, 79
  limitations of videoconferences,
    25–27, 31
  moving hair, 114
  Murphy's Law, 84–85, 97
  negative body language, 18
  no-shows, 99
  preparing for, 77
  videoconferences versus in-person
meetings, 23–24
productivity, 13–14, 36–37
pronunciation of words, 108, 137–164
purposes for videoconferencing, 2–3

Q

Quayle, Dan, 81
questions
  asking before starting, 58
  handling, 56–57, 66
  via e-mail, 56
  See also checklists for managing
    videoconferences

R

relaxation exercises, 110
reliability of videoconferencing, 19
remote attendance, problems of, 25, 28
requirements for videoconferencing, 6
research
  on future of videoconferences, 9–10
  requirements for completing deals,
    14–15
resources, conservation of, 16
respect for audience, 49
rules, establishing, 53, 54, 126

S

samples, storyboard of a meeting, 136
satellite conferences, 13

scheduling of conferences, 61
Schiffman, Bob, 10–11
Scrimgour, Hugh, 32
security, video monitoring for, 131
self-deprecation, 53
sickness, handling, 104–105
slides, 82–83
smoking, 90
software
  overusing, 83
  storyboarding, 48–49, 136
  for videoconferences, 4
  for Web conferencing, 3
speakers, 127–128
starting the conference, 52–53, 127
Stockdale, James, 53
storyboards, 48–49, 135–136
style
  shifting, for videoconferences, 121
  your voice, 109
summaries of closings, 64, 67, 128
switchers, viewing monitor, 53

T

taping the conference, 80–81
tasks, assigning, 58
technical assistance, 69
technology
  capacity for, 47
  contingency plans for failure of,
    84–85
  earliest, 9
  flexibility in use of, 14–15
  improvements in, 10–12
  information technology, 11
  resources for learning about, 5–6
teleconferencing versus videoconferencing, 42–43
Teleportec, 11
TelePrompTers, 76–77
3-D videoconferencing, 11
time issues
  allocation of time for international
    videoconferences, 62–63
  ending on time, 64
  formula for timing presentations, 60

videoconferences, *continued*
   importance of being on time, 98–99
   saving time in future, 132
   scheduling, 61
   spontaneity and lags in broadcasts, 60
   time-saving methods, 12–14
   timing of meetings, 13
tipping point, 16
training for videoconferencing, 5–6
translation services, 62
travel costs, 12–14
trends in videoconferencing, 10–16, 21–22
   See also future of videoconferencing
Tripp, Linda, 117
typefaces, 82

U

unique aspects of videoconferencing, 18–20
uplighting, 78
USB (Universal Serial Bus) ports, 11

V

Ventura, Jesse, 85
Vexcorp, 17
video cameras, 74–75

video images, problems of, 27
videosurgery, 132–133
virtual dates, 29
virtual meetings, x–xi, 20–22
virtual teams, expectations for, 2
virtual visitations, 132
visual aids, 82
voice, using your, 108–109
voice-activated equipment
   cameras, 74
   microphones, 71
   TelePrompTers, 76–77

W

watching yourself on camera, 75
waving goodbye, 64
Web conferencing, 3–5
Winblad, Ann, 29
window lighting, 78
"winging it," 45, 133
wireless technology, 11, 73, 131
women
   jewelry for, 106–107
   makeup for, 102

Z

Zahn, Paula, 93

About the Authors

Janelle Barlow, Ph.D., is president and owner of TMI, US, a partner with the Danish-based multi-national training and consulting group. She is also a keynote speaker and author. Twice named International Trainer of the Year by TMI, she has also earned the Certified Speaking Professional (CSP) designation from the National Speakers Association, on whose national board she currently sits.

Barlow's popular programs, A Complaint Is a Gift, Branded Customer Service, and The Stress Manager, are offered around the world. Her client base includes Hewlett-Packard, Chevron Texaco, Exxon, Mandarin Oriental Hotel Group, Aramark, Shangri-La Hotels, Unisys, Maximus, Genentech, Avon Cosmetics, Paramount's Great America, Dell Computers, Volkswagen, Kaiser Permanente Hospitals, Satmetrix, Southwestern Bell, DHL, and Cisco, among others.

Barlow has written three previous books, including the best-selling *A Complaint Is a Gift, The Stress Manager,* and *Emotional Value.* Her doctorate is from the University of California, Berkeley.

Peta Peter is a senior partner with TMI,US and a popular speaker and trainer. Before joining TMI in 1994, Peter had a noteworthy career in television and radio—both in front of and behind the camera. She was one of Australia's first female television news anchor and also coanchored a popular current affairs program, *Nationwide,* that was the precursor to *60 Minutes* in Australia. Peter has produced award-winning television shows, documentaries and video programs.

Peter's clients include PepsiCo, KFC, Pizza Hut, American Express, Lufthansa Airlines, Toys R Us, Ketchum, Lucas Aerospace, Texaco, and the Isle of Capri Casinos, among many others.

 *Lewis Barlow* currently works in sales and business development for TMI,US. He comes from a background in new technology and on-line advertising sales.

Prior to joining TMI, Lewis was director of sales in Shanghai for 24/7 Media Asia, the on-line advertising arm of Chinadotcom. His clients included Compaq, Motorola, Bosch, and Chivas Regal. Before that, Lewis was head of sports marketing sales for IMG in Northern China. Lewis sold sports advertising packages to multinational corporations. He has a master's degree in Chinese linguistics from the University of Wisconsin, Madison.

■

TMI has grown into one of the world's largest management consulting and training companies with representatives in thirty-eight countries. More than 150 expert consultants and presenters introduce TMI concepts in twenty-four different languages. In 1988, TMI was named the premier training organization in Europe by the European Service Industries Forum, which followed the training of 14,000 European Economic Community employees in a course called "Management for Everyone." Each year more than 250,000 people from large and small organizations all over the world attend TMI programs to learn how to better manage time, people, and performance; to deliver exceptional service and quality; to manage culture change; to brand their customer service, and to treat complaints as gifts.

The TMI, US Web page is at www.tmius.com. All three authors can be reached at the TMI offices in Las Vegas at (702) 939-1800. Their e-mail addresses are JaBarlow@tmius.com, Peta@tmius.com, and LewisBarlow@tmius.com.

Berrett-Koehler Publishers

BERRETT-KOEHLER is an independent publisher of books, periodicals, and other publications at the leading edge of new thinking and innovative practice on work, business, management, leadership, stewardship, career development, human resources, entrepreneurship, and global sustainability.

Since the company's founding in 1992, we have been committed to supporting the movement toward a more enlightened world of work by publishing books, periodicals, and other publications that help us to integrate our values with our work and work lives, and to create more humane and effective organizations.

We have chosen to focus on the areas of work, business, and organizations, because these are central elements in many people's lives today. Furthermore, the work world is going through tumultuous changes, from the decline of job security to the rise of new structures for organizing people and work. We believe that change is needed at all levels—individual, organizational, community, and global—and our publications address each of these levels.

We seek to create new lenses for understanding organizations, to legitimize topics that people care deeply about but that current business orthodoxy censors or considers secondary to bottom-line concerns, and to uncover new meaning, means, and ends for our work and work lives.

See next pages for other publications
from Berrett-Koehler Publishers

A Complaint Is a Gift
Using Customer Feedback As a Strategic Tool

Janelle Barlow and Claus Möller

A Complaint Is a Gift is a "how-to" book for those who want to turn complaints into a strategic tool to increase business and customer satisfaction. Presenting dozens of real-life striking examples of poor—and excellent—complaint handling, Barlow and Möller show that companies must view complaints as gifts if they are to have loyal customers.

Paperback, 232 pages • ISBN 1-881052-81-8
Item # 52818-415 $16.95

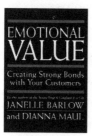

Emotional Value
Creating Strong Bonds with Your Customers

Janelle Barlow and Dianna Maul

Today's consumers demand not only services and products that are of the highest quality, but also positive, memorable experiences. This essential guide shows how organizations can leapfrog their competitors by learning how to add emotional value —the economic value of customers' feelings when they positively experience products and services—to their customers' experiences.

Hardcover, 300 pages • ISBN 1-57675-079-5
Item #50795-415 $27.95

The Knowledge Engine
How to Create Fast Cycles of Knowledge-to-Performance and Performance-to-Knowledge

Lloyd Baird and John C. Henderson

The Knowledge Engine shows that in the new economy, knowledge must be captured from performance as it is happening and used to improve the next round of performance, integrating learning and performance into a continuous cycle. The authors show how to produce knowledge as part of the work process and quickly apply that learning back to performance to create a "knowledge engine" that drives ongoing performance improvement and adds value in every area of your organization.

Hardcover, 200 pages • ISBN 1-57675-104-X
Item #5104X-415 $27.95

Berrett-Koehler Publishers
PO Box 565, Williston, VT 05495-9900
Call toll-free! **800-929-2929** 7 am-9 pm Eastern Standard Time
Or fax your order to 802-864-7627
For fastest service order online: **www.bkconnection.com**

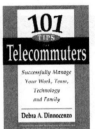

101 Tips for Telecommuters
Successfully Manage Your Work, Team, Technology and Family

Debra A. Dinnocenzo

101 Tips for Telecommuters tells you how to manage your time, balance telecommuting with family demands, and work effectively with others from afar, network the "virtual" way, get a grip on technological overkill, and even resist the ever-beckoning refrigerator when working at home! If you are one of the millions of Americans who wants to succeed in this exciting and challenging new way of work, let *101 Tips for Telecommuters* be your guide!

Paperback, 260 pages • ISBN 1-57675-069-8
Item #50698-415 $15.95

True Partnership
Revolutionary Thinking About Relating to Others

Carl Zaiss

In this book, international business consultant Carl Zaiss discusses the four mistaken beliefs that keep people from building productive and satisfying relationships: seeing themselves as separate and autonomous, relating to others through power and authority, having an either/or mentality, and seeing the world as fixed and predetermined. He offers a new framework that can transform our relationships and, as a result, our individual effectiveness.

Paperback original, 150 pages • ISBN 1-57675-166-X
Item #5166X-415 $15.95

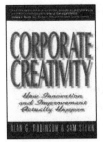

Corporate Creativity
How Innovation and Improvement Actually Happen

Alan G. Robinson and Sam Stern

Rich with detailed examples, *Corporate Creativity* identifies six essential elements that companies can use to turn creativity from a hit-or-miss proposition into something consistent that they can count on.

Paperback, 300 pages, 7/98 • ISBN 1-57675-049-3
Item #50493-415 $17.95

Hardcover, 10/97 • ISBN 1-57675-009-4 • Item #50094-415 $29.95

Audiotape, 2 cassettes/3 hrs. • ISBN 1-56511-264-4
Item #12644-415 $16.95

Berrett-Koehler Publishers
PO Box 565, Williston, VT 05495-9900
Call toll-free! **800-929-2929** 7 am-9 pm Eastern Standard Time
Or fax your order to 802-864-7627
For fastest service order online: **www.bkconnection.com**

Berrett-Koehler books and audios are available at quantity discounts for orders of 10 or more copies.

Smart Videoconferencing
New Habits for Virtual Meetings
Janelle Barlow, Peta Peter, Lewis Barlow

Paperback, 150 pages
ISBN 1-57675-192-9
Item #51929-415 $18.95

To find out about discounts on orders of 10 or more copies for individuals, corporations, institutions, and organizations, please call us toll-free at (800) 929-2929.

To find out about our discount programs for resellers, please contact our Special Sales department at (415) 288-0260; Fax: (415) 362-2512. Or email us at bkpub@bkpub.com.

Berrett-Koehler Publishers
PO Box 565, Williston, VT 05495-9900
Call toll-free! **800-929-2929** 7 am-9 pm Eastern Standard Time
Or fax your order to 802-864-7627
For fastest service order online: **www.bkconnection.com**